Forty Days from the Diary of a Delusional Man

Forty Days from the Diary of a Delusional Man

REVELATIONS AND MEDITATIONS

Jeffrey Hochstedler

iUniverse, Inc.
Bloomington

Forty Days from the Diary of a Delusional Man
Revelations and Meditations

iUniverse books may be ordered through booksellers or by contacting:

iUniverse
1663 Liberty Drive
Bloomington, IN 47403
www.iuniverse.com
1-800-Authors (1-800-288-4677)

ISBN: 978-1-4620-1675-4 (sc)
ISBN: 978-1-4620-1677-8 (dj)
ISBN: 978-1-4620-1676-1 (ebook)

Printed in the United States of America

iUniverse rev. date: 04/25/2011

To my grandchildren,

Benjamin and Delilah

PREFACE

Verbal communication does not come easily for me; however, I found my voice in the written word—that and my art. I can engage in oral communication one-on-one, but in larger groups, my mind spins out of control; I am not able to focus, and I start to feel uncomfortable and frequently speak without considering my words.

The exception to my inhibition to communicate in a public setting is when I am talking to someone or groups of people about art. Working as an art educator with children was something I did rather well. Children don't make me feel uncomfortable in the same way teenagers and adults do. Children are less inhibited and judgmental when talking to each other and older persons, at least that has been my experience. They are open and honest about what is on their mind. They don't discern between the right and wrong way to say something.

I can only speak of the visual arts because that is my area of expertise, but I think and feel that, while art can be well produced, it is still highly subjective and open to interpretation. The artist is speaking through the art piece, in a voice that is personal and not necessarily common to all people. Some of my art is done in a representational style, and the average person can interpret what I am saying because it is technically sound and straightforward. With my abstract art, it takes a person with a moderate to high degree of appreciation of art to understand all the nuances of the particular work.

Although I am not a gifted storyteller, since seventh grade, writing has come naturally to me. However, it took me into my college years to become better at the use of proper grammar. I was always able to say things with the pen that I couldn't utter orally. During my junior year in high school, the English teacher and the history teacher collaborated in assigning students a joint term paper. I got a D from my English teacher because I used poor grammar, but the history teacher gave me an A for the voice I used and the completeness of the content.

By the time I got to Ball State University in Muncie, Indiana, where I was a graduate assistant, working on my master's degree, I had a good grasp of the written word. My communication courses in journalism at Goshen College in Goshen, Indiana, helped me to avoid the pitfalls of run-on sentences that were common in my early writings. I also learned to speak in a voice that most people could understand. This came in handy when I worked on my thesis paper for my master's degree. A number of my fellow master's students wrote thesis papers that were twenty-five to forty pages long, whereas I wrote a 105-page thesis paper on the subject of teaching aesthetics to elementary students. My thesis adviser was totally blown out of the water that I could talk in such length and detail about the subject without repeating myself.

My written communication has not always been well received. I have written some letters in which I thought I was tactful and nonthreatening, but I learned later that it wasn't read in the way I had intended it to be read. Even in writing this diary, I have had to read it many times just to make sure that the raw emotion that usually comes out in my writing was to a certain degree neutralized. I hope that what I say in these pages opens your mind to what people with mental issues deal with on a daily basis.

I chose to write *Forty Days from the Diary of a Delusional Man* in a diary format, even though it is basically a memoir. A large part of the diary entries deal with my past and with the relationships that I have had with people. It is written from my perspective of the events and may differ with what these people think or feel transpired. They are welcome to repudiate with what they read, or write their own book. It is not my intent to be judgmental, and I hope the voice I use is purely descriptive and nonthreatening.

The diary entries are revelations and meditations on daily events and historical accounts of my life. I sought to be honest in the expression of my thoughts and feelings. To illustrate how my mind works at times, I have not always edited what I wrote. At other times what I write will be something that I have written over and over to get a point across. Not everything I wrote is affirmative of the faith I have in Jesus. What I say is what I thought and felt the Spirit of God wanted me to write about, but not all of it is uplifting. Nor is this diary to be read as one might read the scriptures. I do not want the reader to interpret what I have to say as a guide to walking the Christian walk. God and I have not always seen things eye to eye. My life is not an example that I would hold up for others to follow. I make no pretense that what I say in these pages point the way for someone to be holy. On occasion what I write will feel like salt in an open wound. Read with care. Read prayerfully.

ACKNOWLEDGMENT

Everyone I refer to in this diary in a small or large way contributed to its creation. Except for my immediate family and two persons who are now deceased, I have changed the names of all others I make mention of. As for the relationships to some of these persons, I could regret and feel bitter about how some of them turned out, but I do not. I make mention of one person, Dexter, who told me before I joined the army that I had chosen God's plan B for my life. If a person interprets what I write as a tragedy, then he is probably right. However, now that I look back on my life, I am not as sure that God has multiple plans for our lives. I think and feel that everything that happened in my life has and had a specific purpose and meaning, and that it all worked for the good of helping me become who I am.

I want to especially thank my ex-wife, Beverly, for her fortitude and commitment to me for the thirty-one years of our lives together. She gave me two wonderful children, who have become the kind of adults every parent hopes their children will become, in the face of what I was dealing with emotionally and mentally over the course of their childhood and teenage years.

While I feel some sadness that our marriage ended in a divorce, it wasn't wrong that it happened. Our divorce was very amicable, and we are now better friends than we were husband and wife. Simply put, it was time that we faced the fact that we were not able to achieve and acquire the things we needed to be happy as marital partners. Bev endured and took the worst that I could offer any person in one lifetime. She gave her best to do what she was asked to do, and it was good enough; I have only admiration for her. We are both better persons because of our time together, but sometimes you have to acknowledge that enough is enough.

Having gone through a divorce, I now have a different view of the process and outcome. Many in our society frown upon it as a thing to be avoided, an evil. Yes, it is the breaking of a solemn contract. I don't have any plans to marry again, because I am still devoted to the one I bonded with thirty-some years ago. I do think and feel God wants his creation to live a life of happiness. I agreed to the divorce simply because it was the only way I knew for certain that would allow my wife, Bev, to know and find the happiness she deserves.

I also want to say thank you to my parents for the way they raised me and the values they instilled in me. I may not be the religious or spiritual person they wanted me to be or become, but they taught me to cherish life and make the best of what we are granted. Even though my mind has not always desired life, my heart has.

I also cannot leave out my gratitude for the Veterans Administration staff who have contributed to my health emotionally, mentally, and physically. The therapists and psychiatrists have never given up on me when I had relapses and needed adjustments of my medication. They do not get enough appreciation and yet continue to do what is required of them. The media often portrays the VA negatively, and I have my own stories, but overall my experience is that the VA offers veterans the best possible.

Contents

PART II:
TODAY IS FOREVER

Part I

To Forgive Is
Not the Same as
Forgettting

EARLY YEARS

The first three diary entries I have written in an interview style to personalize what I have to say about my past, especially the early years.

16 November

"Jeff, why don't you begin by telling the story of your early childhood?"

"One of the first wars of what would become a thirty-year cold war of political ideals had come to an end. The world's two major superpowers were just beginning what would be known as the space race. In this environment of political conflict I was born, on April 18, 1957.

My parents were the average age for two young people to get married. My father grew up in a farming family. My mother graduated from high school, but my dad did not. Both were raised Mennonite; however, my father had close ties through his relatives to the Amish community.

Mom and Dad met at a youth meeting at her church. He traveled from central Indiana, where his nine brothers and sisters lived with their parents, because there were not a lot of marriage-age girls in his church community.

They didn't date all that long before he popped the big question of marriage. She accepted his proposal because she would soon turn eighteen, and according to her mom, she would have to pay her share to live at home. They honestly loved each other as much as two people could.

My father's father was a Mennonite preacher, so when their day came, they joined their two lives as one at his church. On their wedding night, I was conceived.

I don't have many memories of the early years. I guess our family was a happy one, even though we were dirt poor. My earliest memories were when I was four or five and we lived on a 180-acre farm off State Road 9 between Wolcottville and Lagrange, Indiana. Father did farming part-time and worked in trailer factory full time. I had chores which involved cleaning out the pigpens, which meant shoveling pig dung into the manure spreader and driving it out to the fields to be spread. I also mowed the yard during the summer with a push mower.

By the time we lived on that farm, I had a younger brother. We played in the trees in our yard and on the train tracks that skirted our family's property. Once or twice a week, we would cross the cornfield on the back of our farm and go play with the Catholic neighbor boys on their farm. During the winter of 1961, the snow fall was pretty heavy, and in the space between the pig barn to the north, the chicken house to the east, and our house to the south, there was one big drift. We dug tunnels, built a snow fort, and played for hours on end.

Also, that year my sister was born. The only memory I have of that event was we were trotted off to some great-aunt and great-uncle's home on the east side of LaGrange to stay while Mom was in the hospital delivering my sister. She, like I, was a hard birth. Even though our parents loved all us children, my brother was their favorite out of all us siblings.

When I was five, I was enrolled in kindergarten at the Wolcottville school. Back then the school building was for all grades up to twelfth grade. All of us kindergartners sat on either side of a long table. In first grade we sat at individual desks in rows facing the front of the class. We watched movies of how scientists and engineers envisioned the future to be, with cars that didn't require a driver and homes that had every luxury. Although reality for me was being a member of a poor farming family, those movies fueled and inspired my imagination and delusions.

Every month we had safety drills for tornadoes and A-bombs. Tornadoes I knew about, but the A-bomb was something my parents didn't talk to us children about. All I knew from school is you shouldn't look at it when it first goes off, because the light would blind you, and you should get under your desk to protect yourself from fallout. Also, our president saved our nation from falling into a nuclear conflict with a neighboring island nation down by Florida. It was a sad day when that same president was shot, down in Texas.

I remember we got the day of the president's funeral off from school. I watched the funeral ceremonies on TV. I was too young to really understand what was going on; I had never been to a funeral. The people on TV were all proper in what they did. I was touched when the son of the dead president saluted as the flag-draped casket of his father went by him.

For months after the president died, the news investigated and talked about his killing. Oh yeah, the man who everyone believed shot the president was arrested soon after the incident, and then he was shot by a nightclub operator when they were taking him away from the police station. I was really confused by it all, and it wasn't until many years later that Kenedy's death made much sense to me.

During my childhood, two other important men were also killed by two fanatic men. The one man killed was a black man who was a preacher and a doctor. He was shot because he was trying to get equal rights for the black people of our nation. I didn't know any black people, but the TV was always talking about how unfairly they were treated and what changes needed to take place for them to receive equal rights.

The second man killed was actually a younger brother of the president who was killed. He was killed by a crazy man surrounded by a lot of people in a kitchen. His funeral was more of a private family affair. The nightly news didn't spend as much time talking about his death as they did talking about the first two men's death.

TV wasn't all that important to our family when I was a young child. My dad watched or, I should say, slept through sports games on TV on Sunday afternoons. There was a night when we watched a movie about a spaceship coming to our planet from another world. When it landed, the door opened, and out came a spider-looking creature. My mom turned off the TV soon after that part of the movie. That night I had a bad dream. In the dream I was lying on the ground, and the creature in the movie was walking up my arm. I screamed and woke up. My parents both rushed into our room, and then they laughed because my hand was walking up my arm like that creature did in the movie. We didn't watch many shows like that one again, not until I was much older and could understand that it was all make-believe.

We owned a German shepherd when we lived on the farm. He didn't live to long with us. One day, when I was cleaning out the pigpens, I slipped and fell. The boar pig saw it and made like he was going to attack me. The dog sensed danger to me, jumped into the pen and attacked the boar. He ripped the boar's stomach open and killed it. That night my dad took the dog out behind the pig barn and shot it. He didn't bury it, and several days later, I found the dead dog lying in some weeds with many flies swarming him. He stank. That was the first animal that I loved and saw dead. It wouldn't be the last while we lived on the farm. My mom once brought home a smaller dog, and it lived with us for a while; then she tried killing it when it turned bad. She put the dog in a sack, tied it up to the car's muffler, and gassed the dog. The yaps and screams of the dog made me cry.

My mom many times got mad at this or that, and I didn't like what she did. She especially did not like it when we used bad words. To get us to stop saying bad things, she would take us into the bathroom and rub soap across our teeth. We had to leave it in our mouths until she told us we could wash it out.

My brother and I did a lot of drawing to occupy our time during the day. Once we were so into drawing with our crayons that, when we ran out of paper, we started coloring the carpet in the living room. We got in a lot of trouble for doing that. Mom couldn't get the crayon out of the carpet, and my dad had to buy a new one. We didn't get to draw with crayons for a long time after that.

I was always thinking of things for my brother and me to do that ended up getting us in trouble. On a hot summer day, I found some balloons in a cupboard drawer. I filled them up with water; then we carried them up into a large tree in our front yard that overhung the dirt road by our house. When cars passed under that tree, we would drop the balloons, and sometimes they would hit the car. We did that for most of the afternoon until we were about out of balloons. I dropped my last one on a fast car, and it splashed on the windshield. The car came to a sudden stop, and a big man got out of the car and began shouting at us. He could not see us, but that didn't matter. My mom heard him all the way in the house and came out. He started shouting at her. My brother scurried down the tree and ran into the house. I stayed put because they could not see me where I was birched on the tree branch. Later that night, my mom told my dad what I did, and he took me out to the barn after supper and used his belt on my bare bottom. It was painful to sit down for many days after that whooping. Needless to say I didn't to the balloon thing again but always found something to do that got me in trouble.

It wasn't my first trip to the hospital, but it was the one time I was treated special by my parents. This was when my tonsils were cut out. I got lots of ice cream after the surgery, and we went out to eat, which was a rare thing. I discovered that I loved shrimp, and that was about the only thing I would eat when we ate out from then on.

We lived on that farm until my second-grade year in school."

THE BEGINNINGS OF DEPRESSION

17 November

"Where did you move to after your parents sold the farm?"

"We moved to Lagrange, the town to the north, and the county seat."

"What memories of that time stand out in your mind?"

"We lived in a house that also was a Christian bookstore. My mother managed the bookstore. My dad got a promotion to line foreman in two of the trailer factory's plants. We didn't have much of a yard or big space to play outside, so we learned to make do with the inside space. Both of us boys were in school then, so we got time to play outside there.

The only thing I remember of my third-grade year at school was that the teacher called my mom to have a talk. She asked her questions about what work my father had done before moving to Lagrange. This was because I was telling some tall tales about my father. I told the other children in my class during sharing times that my father had been a firefighter and forest ranger and done many other types of work that made him out to be more spectacular than he really was. I don't know why I did this. I guess I didn't feel or think his work was all that important.

Our family had been attending a missionary church since we lived on the farm north of Wolcottville. It was close enough to our home that my brother and I were allowed to walk to services and back. Two big things occurred during our attendance at that church. First, Indiana had one of its worst natural disasters in the form of a multitude of tornadoes on Palm Sunday. Many people were killed in their homes and on the streets. One report that day was of a man who was found walking around with a wheat straw sticking out of both sides of his head. I also had several relatives who were killed. We went to their viewing at a local school, which was a mass viewing of all the area victims.

The other major event was when we had two guests in our home one night who were members of the Olympic gymnastics team. They demonstrated what they were going to do at the Olympics that year. Their visit made me want to be a gymnast. On the way to and from church, I would do all kinds

5

of gymnastic feats. My favorite thing to do was headstands. I did them so much on the sidewalk that I wore a bald spot on the top of my head, and it would bleed and form a scab, which I picked at for a long time.

I also became a Boy Scout that year. We did a lot of crafts during our sessions. I don't recall what badges I earned. I didn't own a uniform; it was just something I did after school to keep my mom from going crazy trying to entertain us kids.

The next summer we moved to the county seat of the Elkhart county. The town was called Goshen, and I have lived there most of the rest of my life up until now.

The first two years, my fourth- and fifth-grade years in school I attended an elementary school not far from home. Like at LaGrange, I don't remember much of those two years, except for an incident when I fell off the merry-go-round on the playground. I fell under it, and the feet of the children sitting on the outside kept kicking my knee. I was able to walk to class after that, even though it hurt. It wasn't until the end of the school day, when class was dismissed, that I realized I had really hurt it bad. When the teacher said we could go, I found my legs were stuck under the desk because they had swelled up. The teachers called my mom and had her come and take me home. My mother didn't think it was too serious, because all she did was have me lay on the couch with ice on my knees.

I didn't have any friends that I remember while living there. We went to Grace Brethren Church, just down the street from our home. I was baptized there. We didn't get along all that well with next-door neighbors' kids, even though we attended church with them. The only thing that we did with them, when the weather permitted, was throw walnuts at each other over the hedge that separated our properties.

One fall I was given the responsibility of raking the leaves. I took them to an open area in the empty wooded lot behind our house. I was told to burn them, so I got a can of gas and poured it on the pile of leaves; but I didn't untip the can when I put it down some ten feet away from the pile, so the gas dripped on the ground to where I set it. I lit the match and through it on the leaves. There was a booming sound when the gas on the leaves exploded, followed by another booming sound when the flames spread along the trail to the can and it also exploded. Luckily the can didn't hit me when it landed, and because the ground was wet, the fire didn't spread beyond where I had piled the leaves. That was the first but not last instance of my use of gasoline to accelerate a fire.

The summer after fifth grade, my parents allowed me to play Little League baseball. I was a right fielder, but I spent most of the season on the bench. I was put in for one inning toward the end of the season, and I did catch a hit that came out to my area of the field. Our team lost most of the regular-season games; however, we went through the play-offs and won the city league championship."

"You mentioned that you didn't have any friends. What relationships did you have?"

"Well, we were pretty close as a family. We were pretty poor, and we needed to work together in all the things we did. We had close relationships with our extended family, and we spent a good amount of time with them. My mother's immediate family had moved to Florida because my mom's mom developed asthma and needed a warmer climate, so we didn't see them a lot. On my dad's side, however, there were ten brothers and sisters and my grandfather, who was the dominant person of the overall family—a kind of patriarchal figure. So we would spend time with them quite a bit. I had lots of cousin too, and we would do all sorts of things when we got together."

"Did you have any one relative, uncle, or cousin whom you spent more time with than with any other?"

"Yes, I said we didn't do a lot of things with my mom's family, but during my fifth-grade year in school, her middle brother of the five siblings lived with us while he did his 1-W service instead of being drafted in to the army. He was older, but we hung out when he wasn't doing his duties as an orderly at the city's hospital.

I recall one thing weird that he did on Halloween as part of a hayride with the church youth group he was part of. He took a bath in the hair removal product called Nair. He actually removed all the hair from his body, painted half of his body green and the other half orange, and then he greased his whole body to help keep himself warm. All he wore for the party was a pair of green shorts and tennis shoes."

"You said you lived within the Goshen city limits for two years. Where did you move after that?"

"We moved to a chicken-and-turkey farm just to the north of Goshen. We were on the opposite side of the Elkhart Township line in Jefferson Township, so we went to the Jefferson K–12 school. It was to be the last year it was a K–12 school. There were three townships on the northeast corner of Elkhart County that had plans to consolidate the next year, in 1968."

"What was sixth grade like for you? Did you finally start to develop friends that year?"

"It was a difficult year for me academically. Also, it was the first year of school that I have more memories of. I didn't develop a lot of friends until my seventh-grade year, because we lived so far from where most of the kids in the school district lived that I couldn't spend time with them after school.

Our family lived in a forty-by-forty-foot house with a one-hundred-by-three-hundred-foot chicken house behind it, on a three-acre lot. Since our time on the farm north of Goshen, my brother, sister, and I had more space too, but our home wasn't all that spacious for a family of five. My brother and I slept on mattresses in the laundry area, and my parents slept in the house's only bedroom upstairs, together with my sister, who was still a toddler.

In school I didn't do all that well. As I look back now, it was the first time in my life that I experienced a severe depression. I struggled with my studies and even got three Fs and a lot of Ds and Cs. I didn't get along with the teacher. He was creative with how he taught us math and science, but he had a policy of not letting students go out to recess if their grades were below C. I spent quite a bit of time inside that year. Over the lunch hour, I had to work in the lunch area's dishwashing room because my parents couldn't afford to pay for lunch meals for both my brother and me, so I didn't even get to go out to noon recess, which was the only time that my teacher would let students like me go outside.

To help me, my mom attempted to tutor me in some of the subjects. She got me a correspondence course in English grammar to work with. That was about the only bright spot for me academically.

There was also something else that I struggled with, and that was being around people. It wasn't as pronounced when I was younger, but that year I wanted to spend more time by myself. The writing projects of that correspondence course got me started at really writing for the first time. A seed was planted that really blossomed during my seventh-grade year.

Of course living on a farm I had plenty of chores and yard work, and I spent a lot of time outside after school, but it didn't do much for the depression I was experiencing. The bad thing was no one considered the moods I would get into as a mental health problem. I never thought about committing suicide, because that wasn't something that I knew about. No one talked about one's mental state back then like they do today. In my immediate family it was thought to be a spiritual issue.

As I remember, that was when I began to hear voices. The preachers that I heard speak often talked about how we should talk to God and said that he would talk to us through his Holy Spirit. We were also told that we would be tempted by Satan. This is who I thought the voices I heard were from, but I didn't tell anyone else about those voices. It just wasn't done by normal, emotionally well-balanced, right-thinking people."

"Were the voices inside or outside your head?"

"They were definitely on the outside like you talking to me. When I heard other Christians talk about their conversations with God or how they had been tempted by the devil, I could relate and just thought it was something that all people experience. The Bible had many stories that supported what I thought was normal. Moses heard God's voice when he encountered the burning bush, and Saul before he was known as Paul heard Jesus speak to him on the road to Damascus. I was only twelve and didn't know any better. As a child I never came in contact with a person with mental health problems; still, something inside told me that the voices I heard were private and, if I shared what I was experiencing, something terrible would happen to me. I didn't know what, but I had enough fear about what would happen if I talked to others about what I was hearing that I knew I should keep my mouth shut."

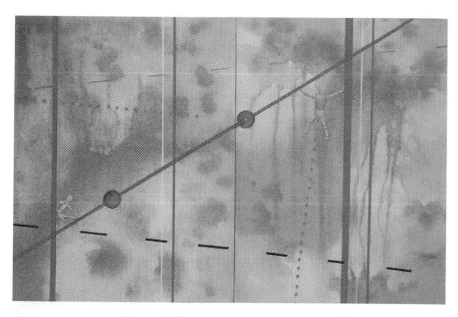

Exercising It
Oil, 24 × 36 inches
2004

"You discovered art as another form of personal expression and communication in your late twenties and early thirties, when you went to college. Could you talk about the painting *Exercising It* and what it was that you were trying to say?"

"Whether it is painting, drawing, or sculpting, creating art is many things to me. In this work, I was perfecting a technique and a style that I started with in my abstract series. With this painting, I first stained or applied a wash of color for the background; then I painted the solid stripes of color for the foreground. The significance of each approach is a representation of the different mental states I frequently find myself in. The modeled coloring of the background for me represents the pain that I experience mentally and emotionally. The more defined foreground signifies the overt face that I attempt to present to the people I have to deal with daily. The foreground doesn't cover the background or even dominate the painted surface, so it shows the viewer that my mental state can be seen by the observant person. The mannequins in the picture portray how I try to deal with these two opposing states of being."

Twin Towers
Oil, 28 × 36 inches
2002

JUNIOR HIGH AND GLORY DAYS

18 November

"Jeff, you said that your sixth-grade year was a problem for you. Did it get better or worse when you went on to junior high school?"

"It started out bad but got better. In fact it was probably my renaissance in school during those two years. During the summer between sixth and seventh grade, I took a math class to help me catch up and be ready for seventh grade. At first I did poorly; then the teacher approached asked my mom one day after class if I had ever had my eyes checked. He thought my acting out in class was caused by an inability to read the chalkboard. The reason he thought so was when I was called on, I would make a smart remark but never really answer the question. I was taken to the optometrist a couple days later, and sure enough, I was told that I needed glasses. After I got my glasses, my grades in that class improved significantly. I was also assigned a seat at the front of the class to get me away from the boys that I had gotten chummy with and who were considered troublemakers."

"Did you improve and have more fun after you started seeing better?"

"I started taking school more seriously. The depression I experienced in sixth grade didn't go away overnight. But one teacher, Mrs. McCammon, found a way for me to deal with my mood swings in a positive way. She gave us journals and told us to write whatever we wanted to write. Another thing she did was open up her personal library, and it was extensive: four large bookshelves of books arranged from floor to ceiling. We were told by her that we would earn an A for every one hundred pages we read. I started reading science-fiction stories and novels. I got hooked on them. This was about the same time that the sci-fi TV series Star Trek made its debut. I was so hooked on that genre that it was almost a religion for me. I saw myself as a Vulcan, and Spock was my mentor into everything logical and alien. I even began to think I was part Vulcan because my ears are somewhat pointy."

"What did you write about in your journals?"

"Besides sci-fi I also took an interest in poetry. Some of my journal entries would be poems, sonatas, and Haiku, a Japanese type of poetry. I wrote some short stories about my imagined journeys to other worlds and the things I did with aliens I came in contact with. Also, I wrote about my feelings of conflict and doubt about religion, in particular Christianity.

Mrs. McCammon never graded what we wrote for its grammar and sentence structure. She was all about us discovering our voice. She responded positively and supportive of the things I wrote. Her approach to teaching didn't mean that she didn't criticize us from time to time or that she didn't challenge us or suggest we think of other things to write about. She simply valued what we expressed with pen and paper."

"Can you give an example of the poetry you wrote?"

"I don't have the journals that I wrote in, but one poem, I remember, is titled 'The Journey.' It goes like this:

The journey
On the path
Far and wide
Near to home
Standing
Sitting
Walking
Running
High
Low
Seeking adventure
Dreaming glory
Across the stream
Under the stars
Off the path
The journey

The poem doesn't rhyme, but instead it has rhythm. Mrs. McCammon thought it had good structure and was very mature for my age. Her feedback inspired me to write more and more."

"Do you remember any of the other stuff you wrote about, like your imagined trips to other worlds or your emotional state?"

13

"One of the things I have always struggled with is remembering details, such as persons, places, and things. I can remember events and stuff that affected me deeply emotionally, but a lot of the intellectual stuff is blown about on the wind.

Mrs. McCammon would reward us by giving us days free from academic work. She would allow us to push the desks to one side of the classroom, get out the beanbag chairs she had in the classroom, and read or socialize. We could do about anything as long as we didn't get carried away or to loud. A favorite thing we could do on those days was go to the ice-cream parlor and candy store that was next to the school building. It was called Vic's. Its ice cream was known in several towns around the county as the best ice cream. It also had all kinds of candy. Some is no longer is made, such as foot-long bubble gum."

"Was there anything else that stood out for you during your junior high school experience?"

"I learned to love the game of chess. I am far from the best player of the game, but at junior high school I was one of the top players. I won almost every game I was challenged to, again, not because I was a master or protégé, but because I naturally took to thinking several moves further ahead than most of my competition.

Playing euchre was also something we did over the noon hour, and again I won more games than I lost, and frequently I would shoot the moon.

When winter weather forced us inside, I would wrestle. A history teacher from high school came down to the junior high during the lunch hour and taught us wrestling moves. I was small for my age but was wiry and more determined than many of the boys in my grade. The reason he worked with us was he was looking to see who he would recruit from the freshman class to be on the wrestling team. During my freshman year, I was one of those recruited, and that season I was on the varsity team as a ninety-eight-pounder, the lightest weight class."

"Sounds like you had a very positive experience in junior high school. Did you have any negative experiences?"

"I came close to dying toward the end of eighth grade. At first, my symptoms were severe loss of weight, diarrhea, and abdominal pain. But other things developed, and my health plummeted. Finally, the doctor had me admitted to the hospital, and after going through five days of tests, he came back with a diagnosis of ulcerative colitis. He began treating me for that, and within a month, I gained back all the weight I had lost, and my bowel movements became firmer."

"Jeff, you mentioned earlier that you experienced doubts about Christianity during junior high. Was your family still attending a church, and if so, was there anything about the church that caused you to question you faith?"

"When we moved to the chicken-and-turkey farm outside of Goshen we found a new church and fellowship of believers to worship with. It was not all that different from Grace Brethren Church we attended while living in Goshen. It was a Brethren church, but behind the name, in parentheses was the word *progressive*. Not all of the churches in the conference of Brethren churches used that word to define who they were as a congregation, just ours. What was different about the church were the ways they worshipped. Instead of sitting in pews, they used chairs and arranged them in a semicircle around the pulpit. They also sang songs that were more contemporary. In the church they draped banners that were to remind and inspire the faithful to scriptural truths. The pastor also was not all that evangelical; he was more intellectual. I actually liked attending the church for those reasons. The pastor challenged us to be like children, questioning those dogmas we were taught to hold as absolute truths and inspired by the Holy Spirit. The youth group was very dynamic and fun to be apart of, yet by the end of my senior year in high school, I struggled with calling myself a Christian.

When I began challenging the pillars of the faith, I also began to challenge and rebel against my parents, but I didn't take on an overt remonstrance until the last two years of high school. I was still dependent on my parents, and they were pretty adamant about the physical and spiritual appearance and behavior of their children. There were certain expectations that I wasn't ready to throw out of the window just yet."

BLACK SHEEP

1 March

Ever since seventh grade, I have felt more comfortable at writing about my thoughts and feelings than talking about them. What I put down in my journals was more real to me than the outside world. The worlds of my diaries, journals, and letters were worlds of fiction and nonfiction, but for me everything I wrote was real. I was safe in these worlds of my mind and heart. It didn't matter if I was right or wrong, good or evil. I simply was.

In my fifty-two years, there have been many relationships with persons and people but not for very long. Except for my relatives, most of the relationships I have had lasted only a year or two. I have enjoyed talking with many of these people and getting to know them, but always something happened or developed that caused these relationships to end.

I have had many relationships but til now the only ones that have lasted have been the one I have had with my family and with the voices. While my dealings with my family have been a mixed bag and frequently tense, the relationship I have had with my voices has been consistent. Even though the voices have influenced some negative actions and behavior, they have always been there, whereas my relationships with people have been fickle and cut short when they felt the need to go in a different direction than the one we were going on at the time we connected.

During my high school years, I became more critical of people. The essays I was assigned to write in my classes and the short stories I wrote for my own pleasure became tools of self-discovery for me. As I look back on those years of my life, I began to see myself as a black sheep. It was an identity that I cherished because it set me apart from those around me. I loved and hated being different. As I have come to see it now, being a black sheep has allowed me to have hopes and dreams that are at odds with the society I live in. All my problems, be they spiritual, emotional, or intellectual, are directly linked to my inability to see the sanity of social norms and mores. In my mind, the real world has been filled with things that I considered arbitrary and conceived for convenience of one dominant group over another or others.

My life has consisted of periods of conformity followed by periods of nonconformity. I would try to live like others, speak their language, do their activities, and play their games. In the end, I would always come to the realization that it all was unreal, it all was shit.

This most dramatically made its debut during my sophomore year in high school in Algebra 2 class. The teacher really was not all that memorable; I will call him Mr. M. However, one incident in that class stood far and above all my other experiences in high school.

It was a class period where two immature teenage boys were throwing paper wads at a girl in the class. This trio was among the elite of our class. I hated their behavior and felt ashamed by the way they conducted themselves, but I hated more the reaction of Mr. M. He had been writing on the chalkboard with his back to the class when he heard the commotion made by these three students. He turned around quickly and glared at them and the rest of the class. The only way of truly describing his reaction is he snapped. He said in a raised voice, "Since you seem to understand the material I am presenting, I will give you a pop quiz today." His reaction startled me. The emotional force that exuded from him overwhelmed me. After he had distributed the quiz sheets, I found myself blankly staring at the questions and problems on the page. The only thing that came to my mind I wrote after each problem and question—"This is shit." I wrote my name at the top of the page and turned it in. Mr. M. looked at the page but not at me. He added it to the other quiz papers.

The next day I expected Mr. M. to return my quiz marked with a big red F. He didn't do that. That day my skin tingled as I sat in class.

It wasn't until the following day that he called me into his small office and sat me down. My emotions were charged, and my nervous system was braced for a very sound rebuke. I was resigned to whatever he had to say to me. He began what turned out to be a one-way conversation, by telling me that he was at a loss for words. He admitted that he did not know how to connect with us. He said that he failed to understand our inability to see the importance of the subject matter. He broke down in tears during his talk. I could barely hold back laughing, as his back was directed toward the large class window in his office and on the other side were several boys making faces.

To my surprise, that day we did connect. He gave me a makeup assignment of writing a two-page paper about why I had written what I wrote on the quiz paper. For the first time during my life in high school, I was in the zone. Most of my life, whenever I opened my mouth, what I had to say sounded awkward, out of sync, stupid, and generally oblivious to what others around me were communicating. I lived in a delusional world. Somehow, often enough, I am in touch with reality, so that I can do what is required to coexist with the others in my life, but there are always those moments when reality seems less than what it is supposed to be. Then my mind shifts to an alternate reality.

SCARS

I just finished watching the end of the movie *Red Dragon*. During its conclusion, the character who plays Hannibal Lecter is writing a letter to a FBI agent in charge of his case, and says, "What a collection of scars you have. Never forget who gave you the best of them, and be grateful, our scars have the power to remind us that the past was real." So it has been with my scars, be they physical, emotional, or spiritual.

On the back of my left hand, I have a triangular scar from when I fell off my bike on a street behind our family's home on Clinton Street in Goshen, Indiana. I had been riding fast down a path through the wooded lot, and when I came out onto the street, I almost hit a car going by. I laid my bike down to avoid the collision, and my hand got caught under the handle bars. The wound, a road burn, eventually healed, but I never rode my bike that fast again, or so recklessly.

There are other scars on my body from events in my life. The largest of these scars came as result of a delusion I had lived in for many years. I acquired these scars when I was in the army, serving in West Germany. I was stationed there for six months, after serving a year and a half at Fort Lewis, near Tacoma, Washington.

The story behind this scar started after the spring term, when I dropped out of college so that Bev, my now ex-wife, could continue to attend Bethel College in Mishawaka, Indiana, where we had met. We started dating after a chance meeting at a roller-skating rink, in an event sponsored by the college. During a girl's choice skate, she came up to me and took my hand. It was love at first sight. I know that it's an old cliché, still it's the truth.

Usually, it's the woman who drops out to support the man. However, I was having doubts about my major, biblical studies, and she was a year from completing her associate's degree in early childhood education. I was three years from completing my course of studies, and I could earn a better income working for my dad's home-improvement company than she could do waitressing at Azar's. It seemed the best course of action.

Soon after we met, I began to visualize Bev and I as a husband-and-wife team, me as the pastor of a church and her as the music director. Bev's minor was in music. During the first year of our marriage, my imagination about our future shifted. The change in my mind came after my dad decided that I would do better serving his company by working on one of the gutter crews. My first partner was Dexter. He was a charismatic personality, and I began to think of him more as a partner and mor as my teacher and me as his disciple.

Because my parents are Christians, I grew up in a religious home. My grandfather was a Mennonite preacher, so I was very familiar with the pacifist doctrine of that church. However, my parents chose to raise us in non-Mennonite churches; therefore, my belief system was not as dogmatic as some believers who live out their lives in one religious creed or another. I accepted believers from a broad range of faiths.

Dexter was different from many Christians I had met. My wife and I soon were attending his church, where he was an elder. The church was what is commonly called a charismatic church, not Pentecostal but similar. The believers raised their hands in song and prayer, clapped their hands, talked in tongues, and prophesied, which was very different from the churches I had known during my youth. In Dexter I saw my future of some day working as a pastor of a progressive, independent, charismatic church. I bought the teachings of his church hook, line, and sinker. Among my thoughts was that maybe someday I would be chosen to be an apostle.

Then one day, while hanging a stretch of gutter on a front stoop of a home in Milford, Indiana, the ladder I was on collapsed. My ankle got trapped between the ladder's legs, and I ended up in the emergency room of Goshen General Hospital looking at two months off the job healing from torn ligaments in my right ankle. While collecting workman's compensation benefits, I had a lot of time to think and watch TV. One day I saw the army's TV slogan, "Be All You Can Be." I began to see that way of life as what was right for me. The delusion of being a pastor evaporated, and in its place, I became a soldier serving my country. A couple of days later, I was sitting in the army recruiter's office signing my life over to a brand-new way of living.

A few weeks after I signed my John Henry over to the army, I got a visit from Dexter. In a few short words, he told me that I had made a poor decision. In his mind, I had chosen plan B of God's plan for my life. That was the last time I talked to him. Two years later, I was sitting on the edge of a softball field at the Landstuhl US hospital, near Baumholder, West Germany, where I had been stationed. My mind and heart were at war with each other, and I was hearing voices that were screaming, "Burn yourself before they burn you." I poured the gasoline on my pants and flicked my Bic.

Initially, when the flames shot up off my pants, I did not feel anything. For a brief few seconds, I was at peace. Then the pain of my legs' tissue and nerves being seared tore through my body. It was not in my mind to kill myself when I set my legs on fire; I simply wanted the voices I heard to stop.

I wasn't thinking how my action would affect my life or others' lives. I did not consider the pain or scars that I would have to live with the rest of my existence on this earth. The future I was not able to see or even imagine. The thought that my superiors were going to burn me was more terrifying than the burning of my flesh.

One thing about scar tissue is there are no nerves in it. Therefore, there is no surface sensation. What the scars on my legs remind me of is that reality is multifaceted. Reality is something that we experience through the countless nerves in our body and mind. The scars repeatedly tell me of my losses but also of my gains. I have lost the sense of touch where the scars are on my body; however, the senses I do have have been enhanced and amplified. At times my increased awareness is a blessing and at times a curse.

The blessing is always with me as long as I keep my focus on Jesus for he restores my soul. The curse I experience when the darkness of my past surrounds me and I feel alone. It's a constant battle or struggle I have to deal with on a daily basis, but what keeps me going is the grace of God.I find myself needing to pray a lot if only to express to God my needs and weaknesses and without him I can not make it.

HONORABLE DISCHARGE

3 March

There is rarely a day that goes by that I don't find myself thinking about and remembering the feelings of June 22, 1983, when I set my legs on fire. When it catches me off guard, it's like I am in a trance. I lose track of time, and all that occurred comes flooding back. To minimize being overcome by what I associate with that day, I have to force myself to do other things to occupy my mind and time. I have learned to do this after many failures, to my regret, and with the help of others.

I got little assistance from the VA for the first twenty-one years after that event. When I was at Brooke Army Medical Center in San Antonio, Texas, I was visited once by a psychiatrist for an evaluation. To the best that I could remember, I told him my story. He wrote up his evaluation and prescribed two meds for my psychosis. When I was finally discharged, I was sent to the VA hospital in Fort Wayne, Indiana, for further evaluation. They prescribed the same meds that I had been put on at Brooke, but my experience at that facility, at that time, was such that I decided that I would not utilize the VA for further treatment. None was offered at that time so I just disappeared off the VA's monitoring scope. I was a peace-time veteran and didn't qualify for many benefits that combat vets got. It wasn't until several years later that I took advantage of the few benefits that were offered.

In October 1984, my DD214 discharge orders came in the mail, and to my surprise the army had given me an honorable discharge. At the most, I was expecting a medical discharge, if not a dishonorable one. The winter after getting my discharge, I enrolled at Goshen College, my home-town institution of higher learning, a Mennonite school. When I first started my studies, I had the VEAP (Vocational Education Assistance Program) benefits that I acquired when I enlisted in the army. It wasn't a whole lot, but it paid for half of my tuition the first semester. After one semester, I was on the verge of dropping out again because I simply couldn't pay the tuition.

About the same time that my funds for college were running out, the VA sent me a letter saying that I was going to be rated zero-percent and wouldn't be entitled to any benefits from them. They gave me thirty days to appeal their decision, so I wrote them a letter, as did my mom. In the meantime, I found a job at the only business in town that would hire me, RAX Restaurant. I had pretty much forgotten about the VA when I got their letter to my appeal.

21

They had reversed their earlier decision and were granting me benefits. I was given a new sense of hope. With the new status, I was qualified for vocational rehabilitation benefits and a monthly stipend. I really hadn't done any praying about it, but it was if God had intervened on my behalf.

After getting my new rating with the VA, one thing led to another, and I was eventually approved for a course of studies to end in a bachelor's degree in art education. During the process of earning my degree, my life took on a new meaning, and my mind began to develop a different delusion. I began to think that there were positive possibilities for my life, that I could have a career and a better life, and that this would prove to my wife that I was once again mentally and emotionally sound and normal. I did not know that my wife had never forgiven me for setting my legs on fire, but I did know that I needed to show she could trust me .

Soon after I started my academic career, I stopped taking the Cogentin and Navane that the army psychiatrist had prescribed. While on the meds, I felt numb and lethargic. They basically cut me off from my emotions, and it was difficult for me to focus or think deeply about anything. I found that creating art and writing, which I did a lot while studying at Goshen College, was a good substitute for the meds. No matter what mood I was in or emotional problem I was facing, I could come to grips with it through my art and writing. It worked for a while, at least long enough to get me through the educational degree program.

Six months after I completed my studies, I was hired as an elementary art teacher for Middlebury Community Schools. With my new job, a new delusion evolved: I began to think that I could make a difference. I was the school system's first elementary art teacher since the school system consolidated in the late sixties. They hired me to write the visual arts curriculum and to implement it in three elementary schools. It was a superhuman task that I felt I was up to, and at first I was successful. The delusion was becoming a reality, but with all delusions there is the possibility of disillusionment and disappointment.

I went through two years of teaching art to kids and had no clue that my ambition and delusion would soon be challenged by a group of angry mission-oriented parents. In the early nineties, a wave of hysteria was sweeping the nation. Anyone who worked with children was a potential sex offender or child molester. One afternoon toward the end of my second year, I was working with a small group of fourth and fifth graders in an after-school enrichment program when the principal of the school came into the room and asked me if I would come with him.

He didn't tell me what for, and to my surprise, all three principals were in the cafeteria with three parents. My skin began to tingle. I didn't know what was coming, but it couldn't be good. Over the course of the next hour, emotion after emotion swept over me. The parents shared a whole litany of ways in which I was subverting their children. According to them and what their children, my students, accused me of was saying things and doing things that were sexually oriented, stuff that was totally inappropriate for children to be introduced to at such a young age. I trembled with anger. I was allowed to defend myself, but what I had to say didn't matter to these parents. In their eyes and minds, I was guilty, and they felt they had the facts to prove that I was a sexual deviant, teaching a perverted curriculum. I felt yanked from the world where I was making a positive and productive impact on children's lives into a world where I was defenseless.

It was a Thursday, and the next day I called in sick. I wasn't sick; I just couldn't deal with the students, especially the ones who interpreted everything I said and did into something that had to do with sex. That's not why I chose the visual arts education as my career. My mind and emotions were totally unraveled, and I found in my medicine cabinet some of those leftover antipsychotic meds that I had stopped using five years earlier. I took more than was prescribed, and several hours later, I was really sick, but at least I was oblivious to the events of the day before. I didn't take any more meds the following day, and by Monday morning, I was in a better state of mind to teach.

A Week later, one of the principals called me into his office and said that all three principals had defended me before the school board, but to appease the parents, they would have to redo my year-end teacher assessment, which I had already been given and signed. All three principals had given me *above average* marks for my teaching and community involvement. These would be reduced to *needs improvement* and *average*. A whole year's hard work down the drain, and I had until the end of the school year to decide if I wanted to continue teaching.

It was difficult to focus on teaching the next few weeks. I did the best I could. In the end, I decided that I wasn't ready to give up my delusion and reason for teaching. I still believed enough in the delusion I had created for myself that I wasn't going to let a small group of angry parents affect the core of how and what I taught to my students. But the next year was nerve racking. I had to second-guess everything I said and did instructionally. It became clearer and clearer that it was seriously affecting my teaching style, which became less inspired.

However, Ball State University's Visual Arts College came to my rescue. They provided me with another delusion: earn my master's degree as a graduate assistant. A graduate degree that does not end in a doctorate is just a glorified bachelor's degree. You really can't do anything with it except mount it in your résumé as an academic achievement. Earning the degree made me overqualified to teach in the public schools. Even though public schools will increase the pay of a teacher who earns the M.A. while teaching, they rarely hire an applicant who has earned one apart from teaching. I knew going into the M.A. program was simply a stepping stone into a doctorate program that I would need if I wanted to get a real teaching job at a college or university. I did it with that in mind.

The thing that persons who live from one delusion to another have to keep in mind is that they are always in a state of flux and conflict with the delusions of others. As I neared the end of my graduate assistantship, I began applying to other universities' doctoral departments. I was accepted at one, Purdue University. Everything was going as planned, and then my wife announced that it was time to stop playing student and think about our children. She and the kids wanted to move back to the Middlebury school district. I was outnumbered. I had started my master's degree a year before but they had sacrificed a year of their lives, so I could get my degree, and enough was enough. My wife also wanted to go back to school and get her B.A. in elementary education.

Another thing I learned about my wife after we got married was that she was always right. Any serious discussion or verbal confrontation usually ended in my giving in. My decision to put my doctoral degree in art education on hold really says a lot about my backbone and resolve to pursue my ambitions and dreams.

LIFE AS A CHAMELEON

4 March

At some point during my teen years, I began perceiving myself spiritually, emotionally, and mentally as chameleon-like. Persons who deal daily with delusions often see themselves as exceptionally adaptable to any location, situation, or relationship. It was rather easy for me to change relationships, jobs, focus, goals, and more. I had no problem fitting or blending into many different social groups. Once I became a physically disabled person it was not as easy to fit in anymore.

When I was first discharged from the burn unit at Brooke Army Medical Center, I was able to walk out of my own strength with the aid of braces. At the time I was admitted to Brooke, the doctors gave me a ten-percent chance of walking again. The nerve damage to my legs and feet was extensive after suffering third- and fourth-degree burns to thirty percent of my body. Having the ability to walk was considered a miracle by many that knew me. While I was grateful that I could at least walk, having to wear braces was a major setback as far as I was concerned. Running and going for long walks was one of the ways with which I overcame the dark moods I frequently found myself in. Having to walk wearing braces put a great grip in being able to do that.

The summer after my burns, I was swimming in my parents' pool. When I got out of the pool, my father suggested I try wearing his high-top shoes instead of the braces that the hospital had fitted me with. I learned that the high-top shoes gave me enough support to walk and appear normal. This was a major improvement. I still couldn't run like I was used to, but I could get around and not stand out physically in the way that the braces made me stand out. I could better blend in with normal people again. The ability to be a chameleon was once again possible. This ability lasted until the year 2000. Around that year, I noticed that walking became more difficult. Standing or walking for extended periods was more painful. I developed a limp in my left foot.

Before my disability began to degrade, like any chameleon when threatened or challenged, I could change my appearance to one with which I could again blend in. For seventeen years, I had dealt with my emotional and mental problems and with my relationships with others, by opting out, quitting, or moving on to something new. Between 1996 and 2000, I couldn't hold a job for more than nine months at the longest, and many were for

25

much shorter periods. Because I could get around like most normal people, I deluded myself into thinking that I was normal. The truth was that reality was becoming too stressful and living the lie harder.

The last normal job I had was working as a journalist for *Goshen News*. As I mentioned before, writing is one of my strengths. It is something that I enjoyed and came rather naturally to me. When I was hired for the job, I was told that I would spend seventy-five percent of my time writing and twenty-five percent of my time doing photo assignments. Around four months into the job, my work assignments began to shift. Photography was one of my minors at Goshen College. I was actually introduced to the visual arts department at Goshen College because my major at the time in journalism required I take a photography course. This was before the VA picked me up in their vocational rehabilitation program. Half of the art in my senior art show was photographs that I had put together for the exhibit. For one semester, I was the photo editor for the *Record*, the campus newspaper. The editor of *Goshen News* felt my skills as a photojournalist were more valuable than my writing, so my assignments switched to doing seventy-five percent photography and twenty-five percent writing. This caused a problem for me physically and emotionally.

I enjoyed the writing more than I did the photography. On one assignment, I was walking across some loose stone and because of the partial paralysis in my feet from the nerve damage from the burns to my legs I turned my ankle and fell. I was carrying my camera, and when I fell, I tried to protect it. This caused me to fall in such a way that I landed wrong. The next day I went to the doctor, who took an X-ray and found that I had cracked a rib. Not only did I have that to deal with daily, but also the journalists at the News worked on the second floor of the building and the only way up was a long flight of stairs. Physically it became so difficult that I had to confront the paper's editor about getting my assignments shifted back to what I was originally hired to do. I guess he saw me as dispensable, so he had no problem rejecting my request for the change.

Not only were the physical aspects of the work becoming intolerable, but also the stress of the job was taking a toll on me emotionally and mentally. I began to hear voices again and began feeling that people at the paper were out to get me fired. One day the editor came up to me and told me that I had been accused of altering a photo that was published in the paper. Photography was becoming more and more digital, and using the graphic publishing software made this easy. All one had to do was simply brushing out a detail that you didn't want in a photo. I also felt that staff at the paper was talking behind my back about my writing. It became clear to me that I didn't belong there anymore and that I didn't fit in with the paper's culture. At the end of August 2001, I gave the paper notice that I would quit in thirty days.

We all know what happened during the month of September 2001: 9/11. Over the summer I had learned that the VA was establishing a clinic in South Bend, Indiana. My physical and emotional problems were getting serious, enough so that I began rethinking my decision not to use the VA's psychiatric services. I sent in my request to become a patient at the South Bend clinic, and it was approved. My first appointment was set for 9:00 a.m., September 11. That day I walked into the lobby and, like most of the veterans and staff on duty, watched the airplanes strike the towers. That day was the end of my life as a chameleon.

LESSONS A PROFESSOR NEEDS TO LEARN

19 December

One thing I have always had plenty of is opportunities. One such opportunity was being hired as an assistant professor of a small Christian college. When I interviewed for the position in the summer of 1994, I thought I didn't have much of a chance at being hired, because of my answer to one of the questions from selection committee. The professorship that I was being considered for was multifaceted. It involved teaching a number of studio courses, overseeing art education majors in the visual arts department, teaching a method and material course for elementary education majors, and lecturing for the department's art history courses. Art history was one of my strengths but not in lecturing on the subject matter. I told the selection committee this going into the interview.

The question they asked of me during the interview was, "Do you consider yourself a conservative Christian?" I had always considered myself many things, but never did I think or feel I was anything more than a plain and simple Christian. The question asked me to position myself on a purely political spectrum, and I didn't think that true Christians took a political stance. We were in the world but not of the world. My answer to their question must have satisfied the committee, for my response was, "Based on my reading of the scriptures, Christians can be identified as being hot, cold, and lukewarm. The latter, Christ would spew out of his mouth, as it is written in the book of Revelations."

Early in my instructional duties, I came to realize that most of the teachers, administrators, staff, and students considered themselves to be conservative Christians. Because I never saw the validity of taking on what is basically a political identification, I went out of my way to avoid the topic in my dealings with members of the campus community. I was successful in doing this until the end of my second year at the school, and then I was presented with a politically hazardous dilemma.

To compensate for my public speaking skills which were weak, in the art history course I was assigned to teach I wrote the course's syllabus in such a way as to minimize students' grades being dependent on their note- and test-taking skills. In place of these graded areas, I gave students alternative graded areas, such as writing, production, and reading skill areas. To earn a passing grade, students needed to demonstrate thorough knowledge of an artist or art movement by either writing a paper, completing an art project, or taking a set of quizzes associated with preassigned readings. At the beginning of the course, students were asked to select one of the above three areas to base their semester grade upon. Constructing the syllabus in this way didn't eliminate my responsibility to prepare for class lectures. Instead it expanded the ways in which I could present the course content.

The confrontation that developed was between an art education student and myself. The course was the art history course. The student failed to turn in her project on time, and according to the syllabus, I needed to dock her paper three grades, from an A to a D. When I informed her of this, she came back with several students to argue for leniency. I did compromise and told her I would give her a B-, but she would not be satisfied with anything but an A. When I wouldn't budge any further, she went to the only other full-time professor and chair of the department and made her appeal. The students that went with her went as far as to complain about my teaching in the course. She also went to the dean of students, who told her she would get an A for the course. I was told by the department chair that if I continued to teach, it would be on a probationary status. Once again my integrity as a teacher was being challenged and drawn into question. The chair of the department told me I was going to be put on probation and would be supervised in the lecture course I was to teach, or I could quit. I quit in anger, anger at Christ and Christians.

I was angry at God because it was in the name of his son that these Christians were doing what they were doing to me. I had another reason to despise the conservative identity that people cling to and I was blind to my own rage. We both thought and felt we were justified in the positions we took, and we both blamed each other for the hurt that was being spread around. We failed to see that we had fallen into the trap of our enemy, who wanted us to point fingers at each other. By focusing on our pain that we were causing to each other, we were not observant to the work of our enemy in us.

Jesus taught his disciples the Lord's Prayer. As a parent, I learned early on that children don't need fancy or complicated things to keep themselves busy and entertained. My son took a box that toys had been placed in for his Christmas gifts and played with it for hours on end, more so than with the toys that came in the box. So it is with the Lord's Prayer; it is a prayer for all seasons and purposes. It is a simple prayer that covers all the bases that God wants us to pray about. In the prayer we ask for forgiveness for our trespasses as we forgive those who have trespassed against us.

If I had obeyed the Lord and prayed his prayer, I may have avoided quitting my work as a professor. Unfortunately, I was not in the praying mood when I chose to quit. I thought I was doing the righteous thing. It's not that

I may have avoided quitting something I loved and felt good at. I may have still quit because I felt this is what those in authority wanted me to do. They just didn't want to be seen as the ones who fired me without justification. If I had prayed as I had been taught, I would have left with a better attitude, in the right mind and heart.

It took many years before I learned the truth that God wanted me to know—that it's not wrong to quit, just that it's wrong to quit when you are in the wrong state of mind, and that you should never quit out of anger. In this situation it would have been right to quit if all parties involved had admitted that it was not the Lord's will that we continue our journey together, that it was his will that we go in the path that he was guiding us to take.

When I was a professor, I thought my role was to teach. Little of God's will did I know, which was that I was there to learn and to teach what I had learned. I did not see the pride in me that blinded me to what God wanted to do in me and through me. As adults we are not that far removed from children, who need to be repeatedly reminded of what is right and wrong. The wrong thing that adults often do with children is teach them to think and feel as adults do. As adults we should look to children to teach us and remind us of what it is in them that God so much desires we be like. I had a professor in a doctoral level class that once stated that the more we learn the more we learn that we have a whole lot more to learn.

What I have learned in my readings of the scriptures is that God does not fill in all the blanks. He intentionally leaves things out, so that we would ask questions. Is praying not the asking of questions? The scriptures give us just enough knowledge that we might see him and his way for us, but not so much that we all become robots, manufactured replicas of him. His work in us is extremely individualized. If everyone strictly followed the law of the scriptures, we would all be carbon copies of the law. It is by the law that we are judged and condemned, but God doesn't want us to blindly obey the law. Rather it is his will that we come to him through his son, Jesus. More than simply forgive us our sins, God wants to transform us by the power of his spirit. Our lives are full of blanks. He wants to give us the opportunities to fill in those blanks.

A Bearable Life
Pen and ink, 9 × 12 inches,
1998

This drawing captures in its title my philosophy for living a bearable life.
I endure accepting what life has given me, for it is enough. I need no more.

BURN YOURSELF BEFORE THEY BURN YOU

6 March

A letter from the VA came in the mail this morning. I had been expecting it for several months, ever since my divorce was decreed by the judge. It stated that, because I no longer could claim my wife as a dependent, my VA pay was going to be reduced.

Our divorce was very amicable, and since both our children were grown and on their own, there was no difficult custody battle. We divided our possessions equally and we went our separate ways. My ex-wife and I are actually better friends now than we were husband and wife.

The event that changed our relationship occurred while I was stationed in West Germany in 1983, when I set my legs on fire. What I did to myself caught her completely by surprise. She was living in Tacoma, Washington, near Fort Lewis, where I had first been stationed. The army did not move my family with me when I was transferred to Baumholder. The reason for the transfer was not because they needed my special skill set in Germany but because my life had been threaten by several soldiers in my unit at Fort Lewis for snitching on their drug use. When I told my section chief of their activities, I was promised that no one would find out that it was I who informed on them. They eventually put two and two together, and I became the focus of hostile retaliation.

I think there was also another reason behind their decision to transfer me out of the battalion. I had begun talking about requesting an MOS change. Months before my unit had gone through extensive retraining to convert us from 13 Echos, cannon fire direction specialists, to 13 Charlies, TAC fire operations specialists. The latter MOS meant we would be computerized and a nuclear artillery unit. Instead of firing conventional rounds, we were then able to modify our artillery weapons to fire rocket-propelled nuclear rounds at the enemy.

When I got my DD214 stating I was honorably discharged from the army, this retraining and MOS change did not show up on the document. The only reason for excluding this from my records I can think of is they didn't want it known that they were training soldiers for this form of warfare.

When I enlisted, I knew that I might be called upon to die for my country and that my actions in the service might result in the loss of lives other than my own. Conventional artillery is a lot more accurate today than it was when first employed centuries ago. The chance of civilians being killed by the firing of conventional rounds from an artillery gun is minimal as long as the correct firing instructions are given to the firing battery. The chance of there being civilian casualties with a nuclear round is far greater. The blast itself might do fairly precise damage, but there is always the radiation fallout. We were told in our training that we couldn't fire a nuclear round far enough that we wouldn't be killed too. We were basically committing suicide. A common saying among the officers to the enlisted was, "Put your head between your legs and kiss your ass good-bye." All this began a long process of my rethinking my chosen career in the military. It's not that I wanted out of the army but rather a reassignment to a noncombatant unit or MOS.

Having grown up in a religious home with a history of pacifist teaching, along with nonmilitary service, I began feeling and thinking that I didn't want to be a combat soldier anymore. Like I said, it was not my intent to get out of the army. I wanted to serve my country as a soldier, but if there was the slightest chance that I could change my military occupation status, I was going to seek it. I did my research and learned that the army provided soldiers with this option, so I pursued it.

When I approached the commanders of my battalion at Fort Lewis about the change of my convictions, I must have scared the hell out of them. They didn't want anything to do with me anymore. They may have thought that a change of scenery would alter my thinking and squelch this new direction I was pursuing. It did neither. In fact, it did more to intensify it than anything else.

Over the next six months, the leadership of my battalion in Baumholder, West Germany, ignored my requests or misplaced the paper work or told me it simply got lost in the process. As I reflect back on those days I feel they doing all this and more to get me to change my mind. What was in my heart didn't change, but the state of my mind did change. Under the stress, my thoughts became more and more confused and out of touch with reality. I began seeing things that weren't there and hearing voices like I did in my youth. It took all the concentration I could muster to just get through the day without losing it totally. I tried to remain patient but I became more and more agitated with people around me. About two months before I set my legs on fire, I began to think that I was one of the prophets that God would send back before the end times and that I would be killed by the anti-Christ. I tried to stay in touch with reality but couldn't, and no one would help me.

I wrote a lot of letters to my family in my free time, but it took weeks and months for these letters to get to them. None of the letters they wrote me got through.

Early in my marriage to Bev, I learned she did not respond well to change.

It took her a long time to adjust to anything new I presented her with, so I decided I would tell her about my MOS change when it actually materialized. But when it came to my parents, and especially my grandfather, who was a Mennonite preacher, I felt I could be honest about what I was going through because I thought they could relate to what I was going through. My dad grew-up during World War II and during the military draft of the early phases of the Cold War. When it was his time to serve his country, it was a simple thing for him to enlist, not as a combatant soldier though. Because he was raised Mennonite, he had the option to join the 1-W service for conscientious objectors. He did his service in Fort Wayne, Indiana, a hundred or so miles from his family farm. He worked on a state farm for what was then called the mentally retarded.

Like I have shared before, I was raised in a religious home, but my parents chose not raise their children as Mennonites. When I was still in my senior year of high school, I tried enlisting the new volunteer military of our nattion. I applied for service duties in the air force, but the new military was more particular about whom they selected for service during its early days. When I was a teenager, I suffered from a condition known as ulcerative colitis. This medical history disqualified me from joining the air force. I did not attempt to enlist in the army until eight years later, when policies and standards had shifted. The army medical staff took a battery of X-rays but found no evidence that I had ever had ulcerative colitis, so I was in.

A contradiction in my life's story is that I spent a year an a half in Washington DC serving as a volunteer with the Mennonite Church based in Lancaster, Pennsylvania. When I enlisted in the army several years later, it never occurred to me that I was in conflict with myself or anyone else by serving for two diametrically different institutions. But then again, I suffer from a delusional mind. I didn't know I was delusional, and neither did anyone else think I was. It simply wasn't a part of people's vocabulary back then.

One of the affects of the psychotic breakdown that I experienced, along with the trauma of my legs being burned, was the loss of memory. I didn't suffer total amnesia, but my memories of that time are fragmented. I don't remember any of the names of those I had contact with in Baumholder. I know them only by their rank. Much of my time in Germany is lost. Only highlights remain, along with vivid traumatic clips of my most memorable experiences.

One of these experiences I had during maneuvers in Grafenwöhr, near the East German border. On a morning midway through the training, I woke up hearing voices telling me to fake being asleep and to not follow any orders to get out of the sack until the officer of the right rank ordered me to.

It turned out that my unit commander, the captain, was the one they wanted me to obey. Later that day, I approached him with a question about if I should be discharged for mental problems, what they call a section 8. He told me that in no way would I be allowed to use that option and that, if I made any further attempts to change my MOS, he would see to it that I would be burned. While I didn't realize it at the time when heard the thousand voices screaming in my head, " burn yourself before they burn you'" it was actually his words that I.

Because I hid the truth from Bev before I burned my legs, she never found it in herself to forgive me. She thought about divorcing me when I was recovering from my burns in the hospital, but after talking with my mother, she decided that she made a commitment to me when we took our vows, for better or for worse. Over the course of the next twenty-six years she took on the worst of me and remained committed. I can only admire her for that.

Before I attempted suicide in September of 2009m, we actually had a conversation about her inability to forgive me. I asked her point-blank one afternoon if she had ever forgiven me, but she refused to respond to my question. I took that as a no. We also talked then about getting a divorce. I finally came to the realization that I could never make her happy and that she was better off without me. I was beginning to understand that she deserved to be happy more than I deserved to be her husband. Unconsciously, my attempted suicide was my way of telling her that she was free to pursue happiness.

It's a constitutional right of US citizens to pursue happiness. It should be included in everyone's wedding vows, more so than the phrase, "for better or for worse." Marriages in our modern society would be much better off if we told each other that our commitment would be based on doing everything in our power and ability to guarantee the happiness of the person we choose to marry.

Bev will always be my first love. I love her still and always will. I believe I love her more now than I ever did as her husband. Although I am sad it has taken me so long to come to this realization, for her happiness I am willing to give up the delusion of our marriage.

DISCIPLINE AND DISCIPLESHIP

21 December

One of the reasons I wanted to pair up with Dexter on my father's gutter crew was I saw him as a person who could disciple me. When enlisted in the army I saw it as a way to learn discipline. Both discipleship and discipline require a person to be submissive to authority. With discipleship the relationship is one-on-one, and with military discipline the relationship is with the chain of command.

When I worked with Dexter, we spent time each day reading the scriptures, praying, and working on the tasks we were assigned. He taught me about walking with Christ in the Holy Spirit. Things were going along well, and Dexter decided to do mission work in West Germany. Although it wasn't an overnight decision from his perspective, I learned about it one day and the next day he was gone.

The sudden change in our relationship hurt me because I was not informed that he was being led by the spirit to go in a different direction. The whole discipleship thing that I thought I had going on was blown out of the water. My father then partnered me up with Dennis who also attended the same church that Dexter belonged to. I could have transferred my discipleship relationship to Dennis; however, he was not part of the authority structure of the church like Dexter. Dennis wasn't led by the spirit to be part of the ministry leadership of the church, so he couldn't provide me with a step up in that direction like Dexter could have. Dexter was not discipling me the way I thought he was, our relationship was all a figment of my imagination, the delusion that I had manufactured.

When I enlisted in the army, I didn't fully know what I was getting into. I had turned my back on God at this point in my life. The delusion I manufactured to justify my enlistment was based on my knowledge of the military via movies and TV shows like *Gomer Pyle, USMC* and *Hogan's Heroes*. While I felt the army could teach me to be more disciplined, I thought that I could get out of the experience whatever my imagination dreamed up. Little did I know that one's imagination was subject to the military code of conduct and that I would not have a say in what that code permitted a low-ranking service member to do.

After I joined the army, I obeyed those who had authority over me. I trusted that they knew what was right and wrong. I didn't question their orders. For the first year and a half, they didn't give me any reason to distrust them. I was a good soldier up until about a week before I set my legs on fire. At that point I had lost all faith in my superiors. The delusion I had about the military evaporated, and I saw them in a different light. I became afraid and paranoid. Everything changed: my diet and sleep patterns, and I spent more time off post at a soldiers' center in Baumholder run by a pastor from the States.

With the breakdown in the discipline that I had maintained up to that point, I discovered that I didn't have faith in anyone that I had known up until then. Everyone was my enemy. I spiraled deeper and deeper into darkness. There were no thoughts of suicide; the voices simply told me to flee, to get out of where I was at. At first the only thing that prevented me from going when the voices told me to go was the lack of a plan. I had no idea of where I would go and needed at least a rudimentary plan before I left.

On June 21, 1983, I awoke with an idea of where I should go. I looked out the basement window of the center where I had slept that night and saw the car of my platoon sergeant parked by the building. I had gone AWOL the day before and knew why he was there. I slipped out the back entrance and began walking to the military hospital in Landstuhl, West Germany. My mind was a jumble of chaotic thoughts. The only thing that kept me going was the idea that I would find help there. Late that afternoon, I made it to the hospital, but the mental health clinic was closed, and that is when everything unraveled.

I did two pen-and-ink drawings of this image: one in crosshatch and the other in stipple technique. The reason for doing them was not so much the subject matter but to show that I could demonstrate a grasp for the techniques used to depict the images. When I first studied photography, it was with black and white films. Learning to get a wide range of grays with an appropriate balance of contrast was what I aimed for in those silver tones. I photographed and printed in the darkroom. The images were realistic. One might conclude that I was mentally well-grounded in reality, but quiet the opposite was actually the case. I saw the images as snapshots of the fantasies that played out in my mind—the perfect image. Reality is far from perfect, yet by choosing the right lighting and composition, I could create the illusion of a beautiful world, the world of my mind.

BLOWN ABOUT BY VOICES

8 March

One of the symptoms of the schizoaffective disorder that I have been diagnosed with is that I hear voices. I go through periods when I can't get them to shut up. Over the last six years, I have gone through a lot of therapy, and with the help of the med, my VA health care providers have prescribed, most of the time the voices are no more than a murmur and mumbling sound in the background of sounds I hear daily. I have learned for the most part to ignore them, but when I experience a high degree of stress, I find them to be annoying, disturbing, and unrelenting.

To combat the voices, I discipline myself to follow a routine that keeps me busy physically and mentally. Each day I do one or two chores around the house, such as laundry, housecleaning or checking my bank account on the Internet. I read some and watch TV. I used to walk, but doing this activity has become painful these past several years, so I go out for long drives in my car. Writing in my journal occupies my day for several hours. After I quit my last job with *Goshen News*, I spent six to seven hours a day in front of an easel oil painting. I had to give up painting when I had no more wall space to hang them and ran out of room to store the paintings in my home. I had two galleries that represented my artwork. Both went out of business three years ago, so I have not done a whole lot with my art since then, other than exhibit them on a website that my son, Brad, created for me. The name of the website is www.hsartgallery.com.

Prior to May 2004, I was working on an abstract painting series. It was one of the most inspired painting series that I had worked on. But while working on it, I became obsessed with thoughts of assassinating President George W. Bush. This obsession and delusion over time devolved into a depressive state of mind. When I began to realize that I didn't have what it would take to kill the man I hated more then anything in this world, I became depressed. When I admitted myself into the VA hospital in Marion, Indiana, I was suicidal. I had made plans to jump off London Bridge. I bought an airplane ticket and made a hotel reservation. I was going the next day and then told my wife of my plans.

Before I spent my time in the acute care ward I smoked about a pack a day, going through the daily therapy I started smoking two packs a day because that was all I could do with the free time they gave us. The habit of smoking also did for me something the meds couldn't do completely, it assists me in focusing my mind so that the voices don't overload my brain with their racing and jumbled thoughts. It is probably not good logic but I have had a number of near death experiences and none of those experiences were caused by my smoking habit. I know I run the risk that they one day may be cause of my death, but I have come to think and feel that when my time comes to die I can not do anything to prevent so I will do what I believe is best for me now even if it is not the popular thing to do.

At first in the acute care ward of the VA hospital I slept a lot and kept to myself, but through the therapy sessions, I got to know other patients. I also did a number of pen-and-ink drawings, such as portraits, scenes with birds in them, and of buildings on the Marion VA campus. Unfortunately, I don't have any photos of that work. I did make more money doing commission work for the patients I got to know than I had made up to that point working as a studio artist.

Since then I have gone through periods every year and a half to two years, when I have had to readmit myself to the acute care ward. It's usually to have my meds reevaluated and adjusted because my body has adapted to the previous dosage prescribed, and they are no longer effective in controlling the voices, moods, and suicidal thoughts. Of all the different symptoms I experience, the voices are the worst.

The voices are neither male nor female; they are genderless. I hear them just like I hear anyone talking to me; they are not just in my head. They are distracting and cause me to sleep less and eat irregularly. Sometimes my appetite is such that I snack a lot between meals, and sometimes I don't eat at all for extended periods. It is also difficult for me to focus, and listening to other people becomes annoying. I usually withdraw socially.

Some people like I who are diagnosed with schizoaffective and manic-depressive disorder go through relapses in their mental state because they don't care for how the meds make them feel and act, and they stop taking them. There is also the opposite reaction, where people become addicted to the meds, and instead of taking less, they take more or self-medicate. I have at times fallen into this way of thinking when stressors became too great. To avoid this pitfall I have learned to discipline myself by using a seven-day pill box that I refill once a week. It hasn't worked perfectly on a couple of occasions, when the physical and emotional pain I was experiencing peeked, but by disciplining myself to maintain the regiment the pill box provides, I am doing much better at taking the meds as prescribed.

Being truthful to myself and those responsible for my treatment is one of the biggest things that I have had to do daily. Falling into a delusional state is so easy. It takes discipline to avoid the pitfalls that come with lying. When

I lie to myself only I am hurt, but when I lie to others the pain is spread around. My history has been one of self-inflicted harm. I avoid as much as I can hurting others, but this has not always been possible.

A year ago I also began documenting my daily experiences with the help of my computer. But I have learned that, when unchecked, the computer can lie as easily as any person if it is given the wrong data input. Recently I have gotten so many different messages from the VA computer that I use my weekly calendar to log when I receive my meds and when they are due to be refilled. I am learning more and more that I have to document just about everything of importance to me because I can't rely on my memory to know what is fact and what is fiction. I write it down in ink, since what is inputted into the computer can be altered to easily.

Remaining connected to reality is a full-time job. It has to be; I can't find any other form of employment, because of my mental and physical issues. I have tried to find something I could do for employment outside or inside the home, but nothing has come of my efforts. I have looked at work-at-home types of work; however, all that I have found that interested me were scams perpetrated on those who are desperate. I have lost money on the few that I thought would work for me. Watching out for frauds and scams is another thing I constantly have to keep up my guard against. My state of mind makes me an easy mark for someone looking for a person who can easily be swayed by something that sounds good. There is truth in the old adage, "If it sounds too good to be true, it probably is."

10 March

Life for me has been difficult, but all in all, I have had it better than many who are diagnosed with mental health issues. From 1985 until 2001, I sought out mental health care providers outside of the VA. I received many diagnoses and treatments; but none got at the core of my problems. What they provided was nothing more than mental bandages. In 2004, I finally got the treatment I really needed in the acute care ward at the VA hospital in Marion, Indiana.

The meds they put me on during that stay calmed me and mellowed the extreme mood swings I had been experiencing but they did not eliminate the voices all together. My relationships before going through treatment were often shallow, and my ability to trust people was not as it should have been. Too many times when I shared what happened in the army, people would stop relating to me. I felt like a pariah. A doctor at the Marion hospital told me that I should be more selective about whom I tell what happened. He counseled me to develop trust before sharing and not share what happened as if I was making a confession. This is how I had treated the experience of burning my legs when telling it to others.

It has taken me a long time to come to grips with what I did and the factors that played into my actions then and since. I have learned that many things in our lives are simply beyond our control and no one is to blame; it is just that they happen, and the best course of future action is to move past the hurt and pain, and strive for a better tomorrow.

Accepting the state of being that I am in continues to be a challenge. Living just for today and believing in my ability to cope and face each day's challenges is all that I can do.

After my last attempted suicide in 2009 and the discharge from the Marion acute care ward I found myself dealing with a lot of emotional baggage. While at the acute care ward, I got no visits or calls from my family. I knew that what I did had greatly hurt them, but I still felt that I needed them and their support. None was given, and I was very sad at the loss of contact and angry at them for cutting me out of their lives.

For a month after my discharge, I stayed at a group home in Marion with other vets. Some had been there for a short period, and others for much longer. It was a good-in-between time for me. I wasn't ready to face the world when I left the hospital. The stay had given me the time to reflect and make new goals.

The weekend after I returned to my home in Goshen, I was invited to my parent's home for a meal. During that meal we talked about the events that had led up to my suicide and my state of mind at that time. The meal was excellent; however, I left feeling deeply hurt by what my parents had to say to me. During our conversation, they were up-front about what they thought about me along with all the things that were wrong with me. I could accept what they had to tell me because I knew of the things that were wrong with me. Where we differed was in how to overcome the issues I had to deal with. They told me that, if I got myself morally right, my mental health issues would go away.

I have prayed that God would heal me and take these disorders from me, but he has not answered my prayers. I don't believe or think that my condition is due to my moral state. It is a physical ailment, much like any disease or health issue. The only treatment for these disorders is medical and psychiatric. Thinking like this might be viewed by some as wrong, but simply put, I am not like most people.

Most of the time, I can act and behave like most people. I know how to fit in to one degree or another. However, there are times when my body over- or under produces certain chemicals that my brain uses, and then everything shifts, often to the worst. The best I can do is take my meds as prescribed, but they don't always work as prescribed. That is why I need constant contact with my health care providers and those who offer me therapy. However, professional therapy can take me only so far. I have found that creating art and writing are forms of therapy that help, along with contact with people. Relationships with other vets as well as people of faith serve to provide a system of checks and balances for me emotionally, mentally, and spiritually.

I think of myself as a moral person. Morality in all cases doesn't work for me when I am overcome with anxious thoughts, depression, and manic mood swings and when I have thoughts of harming myself. When my thoughts become a jumble and confusion overwhelms, all the quaint scriptural sayings become meaningless to me. I can't even pray. The only thing that I can depend on in times when my mind isn't working for me is that God's grace is sufficient.

I was deeply saddened and hurt when my family didn't come around after my attempted suicide. I have a different view of that now. While there is still some pain, I think it was for the best. I didn't see it that way then, and this was probably not what they intended, but looking at the issues I have been facing, the break from each other was the right thing to happen. My family doesn't deserve to be blamed for what I have done. They didn't know what

I was experiencing emotionally and what was in my mind. Very few normal people know what we who deal with mental health issues actually go through. That is why people who are perceived as crazy, have a few screws loose, or are totally off the wall are put away, out of sight from the general population. The thinking is if you can't comprehend or understand it, then don't have anything to do with it. It's better to be out of sight, out of mind.

Slowly but surely, some relationships with my family are being renewed, but it will not be as before;. Our relationship before my attempted suicide were one of ignoring my mental health problems. It will not be so if we are to have relationship in the future.

YOU GET WHAT YOU GET

11 March

I was watching an episode of *House* last evening. In a scene toward the end of the episode, a billionaire is about to sign a document that will bankrupt his company. His advisers are trying to reason with him not to do it; they bleed with him by telling him he is insane and to consider how his decision will affect thousands of his employees. The main character of the show also makes the comment, "People don't get what they deserve; they get what they get." This statement reminded me that I didn't do anything to get what I was handed in life. No one specifically was at fault for how my life turned out or the things I have experienced as a result of my physical and mental health issues. I simply was handed what I have.

What I have done in the past, present, and future has to mean something. I can think of it as a curse or that it's an opportunity to make something good of it. I have thought about why I am writing this diary. Is it a confession to make penance; or do I want to sell a lot of books and make a bundle, or something else? I don't know exactly what will come of writing this document. I have had a range of thoughts about it, but I have learned that until it happens it isn't real. I don't live in a life of delusions all of the time. I experience periods of clarity and conformity followed by periods of disfranchisement and delusional thinking.

As I write, I think of my children and two grandchildren, Benjamin and Delilah. I want their lives to be full and rich with experiences, and the best they possibly can have. The world we live in is far from perfect. As a nation, we face many social, political, and economic difficulties. All of these individually or combined could change the world we live in for the worst, or we could see them as an opportunity to make for ourselves a better world to live in.

I have made my best effort and will continue to strive to improve the world we live in within my means and ability. I want my children to grow up in such away that they will be ready to deal with the challenges they face alone and jointly with their fellow citizens.

The society and culture that we live in is like a body. The heart of the body is the economic system that pumps financial nutrition throughout the body revitalizing its various organs and tissues. The brain is the body's educational system. It perceives and senses and provides those impulses that make the body function properly. The brain and heart should work as partners, or at least that is what I view as the intention of our creator long ago.

This body is seriously ill and in need of a major overhaul. Some blame it on the brain; others blame it on one or more of the body's organs. I think this blame game is a diversion from the real problem. It is our heart that is terminally ill. Religious people often refer to the heart as the seat or house of the soul, while others say the soul resides in the brain. I see the heart of our society to be its economic system. It no longer provides the body with the life-sustaining nutrients that are necessary to maintain a living organism. Our nation needs a heart transplant, a new heart—not one like the old heart, but a totally different heart. We will not be able to get this heart from another donor. Rather we will have to grow a whole new heart.

It will take leadership that can see the failings of the old heart and have the commitment and conviction to make the right choices for constructing the new heart. We cannot depend on the old school of thinking. We must see value in every member of our society and see each person as having a way of contributing to making the body healthy and function properly.

Capitalism doesn't work anymore, and our heart broke itself in its battle to defeat communism. Socialism is a possibility, but we need to improve it. We must see the value in space exploration and not do it for reasons other than economics. Our educational system could be improved; however, we need to stop going through mood swings when determining how we educate our youth and citizens. There is sufficient evidence and theory of how to do it right. We simply need to let those with the vision do it and not weigh how much it's going to cost.

Simply put, we must stop pointing fingers and become actively involved in providing solutions to our problems. No one is to blame. All are worthy to live a quality of life wherein their basic needs are provided for, and all citizens can excel without having to worry about if they can afford the basic needs for living. If they have talent and are gifted in a certain area, they should have a place to do what they can do best. If they want to work with their hands, they should be able to do that. If they are brilliant at the computer, their skill should be put to work. We need more doctors and health care providers. Our farming system is one of the best in the world, but we could always use more farmers. The condition of our roads is horrible, and we need more mass transit. Whatever their ability and means, they should be encouraged in it. This is the world I envision for my children and their children.

We may get what we get, but we don't deserve to be exploited or hindered by the economic whims of a few who profit from the needs, wants, and desires of the majority. We all own this world we live in; it is ours to improve on. If we fail to use the gifts, talents, and resources we have been given to the benefit of all, then we deserve worse than what we have been given. Am I delusional?

COMPANIONSHIP

15 March

After my attempted suicide in September 2009, the VA team that had counseled me on different courses of action said that I should go to a group home or residential care (RC) home for vets. At first I resisted this advice because I had heard a few horror stories from vets that lived in these places. I didn't want to lose control of my finances and other aspects of my life, like I had heard happened to some in these RC homes. But finally, the VA social worker found me an RC home that allowed vets to live pretty much the way they wanted to.

The group home is called "Wings of Freedom." It allowed vets to come and go as they pleased, within limits. Jack, the house manager, took vets who didn't have cars to and from their appointments; he also cooked three meals a day and distributed the meds. The meals were satisfactory but not anything spectacular. The food was heavy in starches and frequently served cold because of the fact that he had to cook for so many vets. Most of the day was spent sitting on the porch smoking, talking, and watching vehicles and people move up and down the street.

Several of the vets had mental health issues more serious than I, and while I could identify with them to a certain degree, the fact that I was higher functioning made it difficult at times to relate to them. I knew after the first week that I didn't want to spend more than a month or two at this home.

After the third week at the home, I called my wife to see how she was doing and what the status of our divorce was. I learned that she was going to stay with my parents and that I could move back into our home in Goshen. I gave Jack notice that I would be leaving at the end of the month.

During the last week at the group home, I put an ad in two local papers in Elkhart County for a live-in companion. While I was ready to move out of the RC home in Marion and get back to where I was more comfortable, I felt that living alone was not the best idea. I interviewed three people who lived in Elkhart County; however, in the end, I chose Dan, who had been living at the RC home for over a year.

Over the course of the month that I lived at Wings of Freedom, I got to know Dan, an ex-Marine, who was around sixty-three years old. We had gone out for several meals together, and I felt I had more in common with him than with the other people I had interviewed for the companion position. He turned out to be a great cook. Over the course of the three months that he lived with me, I got some of the best meals I had had in a long time. My ex-wife was a good, but average, cook. Dan had a wider range of things he could cook. His only weakness was house cleaning. I renegotiated our arrangement, so that I did the house cleaning and he took on other responsibilities. The overall arrangement was he got to stay in the basement living space for no rent in exchange for his services.

Three months after coming to live with me, Dan wanted to move back to his hometown, South Bend, Indiana. He had friends there, and it had been difficult for him to adjust to Goshen. I was sad that he wanted to leave because we had gotten along so well, but I couldn't begrudge him for wanting to be where he felt more at home. I was even more saddened when I learned that he had a heart attack and died two days after he had left. He had become a good friend, probably the best friend I had had in more than a decade.

I had such a good experience with Dan that I wasn't ready to live on my own just yet, so I advertized for another live-in companion. The first time when I placed the ad, three months prior, the economy was still struggling from a recession that had been going on for a year and a half. There were a number of people looking for an opportunity to make what money they had stretch farther. When I placed the ad this time, those that I had to select from were fewer, and most of them I rejected after a two-minute conversation over the phone. However, one lady stood out. I made an appointment to meet with her. When Barbara arrived she had one of her ex-bosses with her. I didn't think anything of it, although it was a little unusual to bring a former supervisor to an interview. It should have triggered more questions from me, but I was still new at the interviewing process.

After checking out Barbara's references, all of whom spoke highly of her, I told her that she could move in. During the interview, she told me that she had moved back to Goshen after spending ten years in Alabama taking care of her ailing stepfather, who had died two weeks prior. When she moved in, she brought quite a bit of stuff, most of which was in plastic garbage bags and a few large boxes. It took only two days of living with her to learn that she and her references had not told me the whole truth about her state of mind. I soon learned she was still grieving and in a deep depression. I was willing to give her some time to adjust before doing the duties I asked of her, but during those two days, she spent most of her time asleep during the day and awake at night. It became apparent that, if she continued to live with me, I would end up being her caregiver, and I was not emotionally or physically up to that task.

I finally confronted her and asked if I could take her to the hospital, where she could get the help she needed. She refused. Not knowing what to do, I called her ex-boss, who tried talking to Barbara on the phone. She wouldn't talk with her and hung up. I called her ex-boss back again, and after a lengthy conversation, we agreed I needed to call the police for assistance. When they arrived, they spent some time with her and searched through her possession in the basement. At one point, they gave her a breathalyzer test, and it showed her blood alcohol level at .16, twice the legal limit. The police officers finally told me I had two choices: ask her to leave, and if she refused, they would arrest her for trespassing, or if she left on her own, they would arrest her for public intoxication. Barbara finally chose the latter. I learned the next day that she had been taken to an area hospital, where she was being treated for high blood pressure, depression, and a few other medical conditions.

While Barbara was with me, I also learned that she had lived at four places since coming back to the Elkhart County area. She also told me that the reason her blood alcohol level was so high was because she had been drinking cough syrup, but the police in the search of her possessions found several prescription bottles, all for treating depression, along with a fifth of vodka. When I went down the basement to see how things were, I found that she had taken food items out of the refrigerator, and after only partially eating them, left them lying all over the place. Her living area was a mess. What I learned from the brief experience with her is that favorable references sometimes have ulterior reasons. In the case with Barbara, they wanted what was best for her, but did not want to be responsible for her, so they pawned her off on me.

A couple of days after Barbara was gone, I got a call from a man I will call Sam. He came over for an interview for the companion position, and up-front he told me that he had a felony record. The crime he was convicted of back in the midnineties he had done his time for. For most people I guess this would have been a red flag. I'm not like most people. I have been given many chances in my life, and for this reason, I like to give people the chance to prove themselves and do not put a lot of weight on their past.

Sam came to live with me a week after the interview. It gave me time to check his references, who all spoke highly of him. They even said that he was actively involved in their church and participating in a group of people who were working through various past problems in their lives. Sam's pastor told me that the church had a covenant they asked all their members to live by, and Sam lived above and beyond this covenant. I knew his pastor from Goshen College and had no reason to doubt him.

Sam was a nice person. He was kind and thoughtful and took criticism well when I gave it. However, he did not perform his duties and services to the level I expected or desired of him to do. After three weeks with me, I began thinking that I would have to tell him to leave, and so I did. He took it fairly well, even though I could see he was disappointed.

I gave Sam a month to move out. One of the things that I made clear in my ad in the local papers was that the companion must have a full- or part-time job or be on Social Security benefits. They must be able to pay their share of the grocery bill. Sam told me during the interview that he did not have a job but was promised work in couple of weeks. This job never materialized, which was the other reason I had to ask him to leave. Because he didn't have a job and no place to go, I told him that I would give him a month to move out and, until that time, I would not expect any services from him, but he would have to find a way to pay for his groceries. It took him two weeks to get food stamps. Until then, I paid for his groceries.

My experience with Barbara and Sam led me to the conclusion that it was time that I live on my own. During the last month with Sam, I discovered that I can do a fair job at cooking and all the other things I had asked my companions to do for me in exchange for free accommodation. I learned to organize my week so that I did a little each day. This kept me busy. I wasn't lying around watching TV all the time. All in all, this period of my life was good for me.

THANKFUL FOR PAIN

17 March

Today has been somewhat more painful than most days. I woke twice during the night with stabbing and burning pain in my legs and feet. Yesterday I was on my feet more than usual, which sets me up for at least twenty-four hours of pain and discomfort. To avoid these days, I try to balance the time on and off my feet.

I didn't have this problem when I was first discharged from the burn unit at Brooke Army Medical Center. The pain is caused by the way the nerves in my legs and feet work. My left foot and ankle give me the most pain. Over the past nine years, the tendons in my ankle and foot have been stretching. When I walk without my shoes, I walk on the outside edge of my left foot. I can't get it to flatten out.

Several times I have fallen in the shower when standing or getting up from the built-in seat. Once I fell so hard that I bent the faucet handle.

I have fallen while walking more times than I can count. Even since I started wearing braces again, I have had some hard falls. Turning sharply when walking, or walking on uneven surfaces, snow, or ice, causes me to lose my balance, and down I go.

I don't know if the pain is good for me or not. It tells me I am very much alive, and I guess I should be thankful for that fact. Still, it eats away at me emotionally, as a constant reminder of what I did to myself so many years ago.

When the pain started increasing back in 2000, it was still tolerable. By 2004, I could barely walk because of it, which is when the VA primary care physician prescribed morphine for the pain. It was a godsend at the time. They had me on a low dosage at first but had to increase it as my body adjusted to the dosage they prescribed, and with the increases I became more addicted to it. On my birthday, April 18, 2006, the consequence of being on morphine for so long occurred. I felt the need to have a bowel movement but nothing came out.

At first it just was a sharp pain in my gut and lower back; then I looked at my stool, and it was all red. I didn't think anything of it the first three times I tried to go the bathroom, but on the fourth attempt the pain wouldn't subside. I called my wife, and ten minutes later we were on our way to the hospital. Once at the hospital, they put me through a battery of tests. At some point in

51

this process I lost consciousness. The next thing I remember is waking up in the intensive care unit with a large bandage on my stomach and a tube down my nose and throat.

When the doctor finally came in, he told me how lucky I was. He explained that my large intestine and part of my colon had ruptured and that they had removed twenty-five pounds of intestine and stool. He said I nearly died on the operating table and the risk of complications was high because of the possibility of infection. He gave me the good news last. They had been able to fix me up so I could go the bathroom as normal. My ex-wife had told them that is what I would want. The doctor also told me he thought that the morphine was the culprit for my intestine becoming obstructed.

I eventually did have complications from an infection in my small intestine, and they did the alternate surgery. I wore the bag for three months; then they went back in and removed the bag.

When I experience pain like I am today, I have to continually remind myself that I have so much to be thankful for. Pain or no pain; there have been enough good things in my life to compensate for the not-so-good things.. Like I said in my diary two days ago, things happen; we get what we get. It's easy to put blame here, there, or anywhere. In the end, it's simply a happening, not necessarily good or evil. It just is.

No Fear
Oil, 18 × 24 inches
2001

This painting portrays the independent spirit of this then young lady who was my son's girlfriend. She appears somewhat shy, but she is ready to take on the world. She is naive to the hazards that await her; however, she is confident in her ability to overcome any obstacle. This painting is a portrait of my life. I have been down so often, but I eventually get up and struggle to overcome my fears.

LIFE'S CHOICES

21 March

"There are times when the only choices you have left are bad ones" is a line from the TV series *Fringe*. I have difficulty agreeing with that statement. Rather I think and feel we are presented with options and opportunities. I have made a lot of choices which seemed right at the time but later turned south or sour. Also, I have made hasty choices that in some cases were the right thing to do and sometimes required that I back up and start again.

The point to life is that it is one great big learning process or opportunity. You take days or forever considering whether or not you are going to do this or that, or you can go with your gut feeling. For whatever reason, sometimes you are not given all the facts, and you simply have to make your best guess. Of course we all know that life sometimes gives us only lemons when what we would like is apples. Most of us do the best we can do with what we are given.

The mental health issues that I am being treated for are schizoaffective and bipolar (manic-depressive) disorders. Last spring I began having minor seizures, and after experiencing almost a dozen of them, I had a grand mal seizure where I lost consciousness for about two hours. It scared my wife because the symptoms began in a restaurant with several minor seizures, and then, when we were in the car driving home, the big one happened.

About a week after the grand mal occurred, my VA primary care physician had an MRI done of my brain and found a dark spot that suggests I had a ministroke sometime before the seizures started. A neurologist at the Fort Wayne VA hospital concluded that the antipsychotic med I had been taking since my admittance to the VA hospital acute care ward in 2004 was partially the cause for the seizures and possibly the stroke as well. He took me off the med, and within a week, I became manic.

I didn't realize that I had become manic, because the meds I was on had pretty much eliminated the manic-depressive swings. While in a manic state of mind, I made several poor financial choices with my credit cards. I charged my credit cards to there max. When I finally realized what was going on, I was seriously in debt.

My credit rating plummeted, and I had to seek the help of a credit management company. In the process I became seriously depressed and, after a while, began to see my life as meaningless and pointless. Then I attempted suicide. At the time it seemed the only choice I had left. Of all the people I sought help from, none were willing to offer it. I had dug myself a hole so deep that I couldn't see the sky above. I was literally in a very dark place; some might call it hell. Hanging myself seemed to me at the time to be one way out of that hole. I am still working at climbing out of that hole.

Because I made financial choices that left me deeply in debt, the VA sent me a letter stating that they were considering declaring me incompetent to handle my VA finances. I had been working at getting myself help with my finances and was doing a fair job handling my finances after being discharged from the VA hospital. I was at a loss for words when I read the letter. They also stated that I could request a personal hearing to provide any evidence to my defense. So I did.

Yesterday, after a few months of waiting for the reply to my request for a personal hearing, a letter came telling me when my personal hearing had been scheduled. During the last therapy session, my VA social worker said that I probably wouldn't hear any more about the incompetency thing since, concerning my ability to take responsible action for my finances, all the psychiatrist's and social worker's reports had been in my favor. However, this was not the case.

For years I was a credit card junky, getting in debt and then paying it off. I was always able to clear my debt, but I always found myself sucked back into the temptation to abuse my credit. I deluded myself into thinking that I was always in control of my spending.

Last summer's experience woke me up, and I had to face who I was with regard to my financial identity. It will be a long process getting out of debt and changing my spending habits. As with any long-stemming habit, there probably will be setbacks, but I think I am now making better financial choices and decisions. I am facing my demon. I don't know what the VA will finally decide about my status, but I hope I will be permitted to continue to manage my finances with the assistance of a financial adviser. If I don't deal with my demon, I will never overcome it.

Leopard in a tree
Oil, 18 x 24 inches
Commissioned for a friend of my daughter

CONFUSION, DESPAIR, AND PRAYER

23 March

I continue to wrestle with the *why* for this diary. I feel exposed and raw before the world. I am placing myself out there to be judged and exploited. My mind spins with thoughts of how others have taken advantage of me or terminated their relationship with me when I spoke the facts of my life as I know it. Today is a glimpse into my mind when my thoughts have no cohesion.

Nothing much makes sense anymore. I try to deduce the logic of a thing; still all that comes to mind is *Why I am here? Where should I go next? Whom should I trust when all who have known me see only the destruction of my life?*

There are no easy answers anymore. *Who will hear my questions in the darkness that surrounds me?* I beat my head against a wall of stone, and all that comes down upon me is straw. I sneeze.

There once were possibilities, adventure, and delirium. Now there are bills of lading and debtors up the kazoos. I knew what I wanted; my imagination guided me to fanciful places.

My accusers are like the ants to a bloody wound. The sores on my once beautiful flesh are open and festering. I call for a doctor. One comes. Then he walks away. I am still in pain.

Falling, falling, falling. I see the ground; it is so far away. The pictures in my mind are bright and gay; in the darkness, they do not penetrate the gloom. I am overcome. My heart beats time to a drum that is made of tin.

Can I really know the one they call Creator? Is he my Father? How many fathers have lain beside the cave I come from? The autopsy will never be complete until I am reborn.

There is much that can be done, must be done. Will it ever get done? In a hundred thousand lifetimes, the place of our birth will still be polluted from the sorrow that we bring to the dung heap.

Just knowing there is the element of predictability, I am caught off guard. Bravely we go to death's door, lifting our hands and scraping our feet. We rejoice when evil is turned upside down; it's still alive.

I once knew the path that came to me, but to the horizon, I could see no further. The trees sway against the current; their roots are stuck in my ass. I have been cut off from my only love.

Despised among the bastards and bitches, the only friend I have wants my tithe. Raw! I play with him. He knows me better than my mother. He jumps with excitement at the thought of herds of sheep caught on the cliff's edge.

Something should be said of the dawn toreador wandering in the music. Blessed is the toilet seat that I frequent more and more each day. What goes in doesn't always come out. Track marks line the edge of my bed.

Hallowed be thy name. Thy name is hallowed in the tree's trunk. Upon it hangs one you called son. You say I am his bride, but he is absent from my bed chamber. It is said he is alive and will come again. When? I am no young chicken.

Magic and vivid dreams abound my waking eyes tomorrow. There still is a dove in the stove pipe. It once flew from a hand to a rocky shore after much rain. It carried a palm branch in its talons that gouged out my finger nails.

Will the holy of holies strike me dead if I lay in its shadow? A storm swirls overhead.

Rain drops fall on distant lands while I walk on parched leaves. I hear a hammer banging on my toe. Take this cup from me.

Construction Memories
Oil, 28 × 40 inches
1993

This day's diary entry is an example of how my mind thinks, feels, and perceives. It jumps around, at times makes sense, and at other times is nonsensical. This is one reason I am afraid to talk: if I write I can more clearly see what's going on in my mind and make corrective choices.

Part II

Today Is Forever

FEARED

28 March

When I was discharged from the Marion VA acute care ward after my last attempted suicide in 2009, I was driving back to Goshen with my father to pick up a number of items that I needed for my stay at the RC home in Marion. The reason my father was with me is my wife and family did not want me to be alone in my own home, where my soon to be ex-wife was still living. They really didn't want me to return to Goshen to live; it was too close for comfort. During that drive, my father and I talked about many things. One thing he told me was that my mother, sister, and wife had told him that they feared me. Learning this was like a knife cutting across my heart. I still experience pain from that wound to this day. I keep asking myself what I did do to make them fear me. I know I didn't threaten them verbally or do anything to harm them. What is it that causes people to fear people like me?

Since that day, I have come to the understanding through the therapy and education at the VA hospital and though my own research on the Internet that it's a simple principle that has caused this fear in normal people for thousands of years. It's a principle made up in part of superstition and in part of reason or rationalization. In general, people fear that which they do not understand or cannot control with their wit and physical effort.

Mankind has attempted to explain the workings of the mind religiously and scientifically, but they still fear it because, when it comes down to it, they are still ignorant. In the Holy Scriptures are stories of men who were deeply depressed (Job) and those that God caused to suffer mentally (king of Babylon for his persecution of God's chosen people, the Jews). The ancient Greeks also had their stories of men and women who were driven mad by the gods and goddesses for their sins against the gods. Other religions and cultures, such as the Romans, viewed mental defects or afflictions, such as seizures, as meaning that the individual was blessed or had a special relationship with their gods.

For centuries people thought of mental illness to be a state of demonic possession; when I talk about hearing voices, people almost immediately associate that state of mind as good and evil spirits actually talking to me.. In church I learned that we could talk to God and that his adversary, Satan, tempts men and women to do things they would not normally think of doing. It is the easy answer to think that the voices are from an external enity, but what is really occurring is my mind is not working in the way it was designed by God to work..

To digress a little, when I was in my early teens, an uncle on my mother's side of the family wrote a letter to my mother stating that she and I would be attacked by demons. I do not know all the details surrounding that letter, but I recall that my parents thought that this particular uncle was strange. As a young man, hearing things like that from adults you respect has a big impact on how you think and feel about something.

As a child and young man, I thought that these voices I heard meant that I had a special relationship with God, and I could rationalize this because of the things I heard adults around me describe about God and his relationship with us. Our culture does a lot of things to instill and feed the mania and depression that I know now is not spiritual but a chemical imbalance in the brain. This doesn't mean that I don't hear voices anymore; rather I am conscious that these voices are the way my mind functions and that it is not normal for most other people. But I know I am not alone, that others experience this state of mind.

Beth A. Bollinger, MD, in *The Gale Encyclopedia of Mental Disorders*, writes,

> Hippocrates, a Greek physician who lived around 400 B.C. and is regarded as the source of the Hippocratic Oath taken by modern physicians, first introduced the concept of disturbed physiology (organic processes or functions) as the basis for all illnesses, mental or otherwise. Hippocrates did not describe disturbances of the nervous system as we do today, in terms of a chemical imbalance or a low level of neurotransmitters (neurotransmitters are the chemical messengers sent between brain cells). Instead, he used the notion of an imbalance of "humors." Humors were defined as bodily fluids, and were believed to be influenced by the environment, the weather, foods, and so on, producing various imbalances in a person's state of health. Hippocrates' theory was an early version of the idea that physiological disturbances or body chemistry might play a role in the development of mental illness. Most importantly, perhaps, Hippocrates' concept placed mental illness on the same footing as other medical disorders by highlighting the belief that the mentally ill are genuinely suffering, and therefore

to be treated like other sick persons rather than as moral degenerates. Sadly, modern society has not fully overcome the tendency to stigmatize persons with mental disorders http://www.healthline.com/galecontent/mental-disorder. Hippocrates' more "enlightened" perspective, however, meant that someone with depression http://www.healthline.com/adamcontent/depression or schizophrenia http://www.healthline.com/adamcontent/schizophrenia could be viewed as being in a state of "disease," just like a diabetic http://www.healthline.com/adamcontent/diabetes or someone with high blood pressure.1

I said earlier that my father told me that the female members of my family had told him that they feared me. It hurt to hear this, but I should not diminish the emotions they experience when around me. At times I can be unpredictable. While I have not done anything to suggest I would ever harm them, this doesn't mean that, if the condition in my mental state changed suddenly, I might do something that might be perceived as a threat. I do not like to think of that possibility, but I have learned that preparation and education are the best defense against the improbable change in my mental state. What do I do if I find myself thinking about harming someone other than myself? The first and foremost thing that I need to do is call my mental health care provider right away. Second, I need to remove myself from the environment that I am in, get out of the house, and admit myself to the VA hospital—anything that puts space between me and the conditions that are overwhelming me. I actually did this a couple of years ago, when I realized that I was overwhelmed with thoughts of harming my now ex-wife. The thoughts and emotions came out of the blue, but I knew that I could not deal with them on my own.

When I was discharged from the VA hospital this last time, I knew that living alone was not the answer, even though I wanted to crawl into a hole and die. The group home provided me with some companionship for the short term, but staying there was not the answer for the long term. I needed to know that I could survive on my own. The next natural step was to take on a live-in companion. Each of the companions that I have had these past six months has provided me something that has built up my confidence. This being that I could survive cycles of emotional storms and come out the other side a stronger and better person.

The *Laundress* is representative of my need for stabilizing companionships in an environment that is like a strong wind. In the painting, there are strong verticals and horizontals in the trees and wood siding; these provide rhythm

---

1   *The Gale Encyclopedia of Mental Disorder.* s.v. "Hippocrates"

and balance. The sheet blowing the wind behind the laundress acts as dynamic focal point.

Laundress
Oil, 18 × 24 inches
2001

PEACE, BE STILL

2 April

I woke up early this morning at 3:00 a.m., finding myself thinking about the ancient scripture passage, "Yea, though I walk through the valley of the shadow of death, I will fear no evil; for ... thy rod and thy staff, they comfort me," of Psalm 23. While I have difficulty at times in calling myself a Christian, I still find comfort in those passages written so long ago by men who submitted themselves to the will of God.

I find it difficult to call myself a Christian because of all that I have gone through and the way some Christians have treated me in the past. However, I must be truthful; with all the pain that those who call themselves Christian have caused me over my lifetime, I still feel that the God of those ancient writers cares about me and has a purpose for my life. The teachings of Jesus of Nazareth echoes in my mind as I walk this road I am on. In one way, I am still his follower and therefore a Christian. If not for the grace of the Father of Jesus, I would have been overcome by evil long ago.

After telling someone close my life's story, she commented that I am under a curse. If this is so, it is my desire that these persons would come out of the shadow into the light, where I could confront them, and given the opportunity, I would ask for their forgiveness for whatever sins I have committed against them and tell them that I wish them no ill.

Love is a difficult thing for me to control emotionally. It has so many meanings and manifestations. It is in many ways a delusion that I find myself overcome by at times, like being on a stormy tumultuous sea. Like the story of Jesus's disciples in a small boat being tossed around by the winds and waves. Suddenly they see Jesus coming to them walking on the water. Peter calls to Jesus, and the Lord beckons him to get out of the boat and walk to him. Peter does this, and for a time he too is walking on the water, but then he sees the tumultuous water around him and begins to sink. Often I find myself, like Peter, sinking and unable to see the possibility of Jesus standing there with his arms outstretched and saying, "Peace, be still."

I have always been one who wants to get out of the boat and walk on the water. I know that this is a delusion of my mind. I have always been impulsive. Jumping in without weighing the risk or the controversy I may cause is part of my nature. For brief periods of time, I can tell myself to wait, wait, wait; but then the urge exceeds my ability to stay put any longer. My heart is most often the organ I follow, even when my brain is telling me that it does not make any sense or that it is not a wise thing to do.

A puddle of water for me is not just a puddle of water, but a raging tempest caused from my stomping on it. Most people would leave that puddle alone, walk around it. For me it is a mighty ocean, full of danger and possibilities.

Lately, I have been thinking about what I will say at my personal hearing next Tuesday, down in Indianapolis, in front of the VA committee which is considering declaring me incompetent to handle my finances. What can I say that will give them confidence in my ability to manage the money they provide me to live on? One thing my training in the visual arts has taught me is how to see things, be they animate or inanimate, from different perspectives and to look at issues both objectively and imaginatively. It is very easy for me to see myself as those on the committee might see me. It's not hard for me to imagine that they would see me as someone who uses poor judgment in the overall handling of his income. However, I think I am learning to do better in making financial decisions. Over the last six months, I have had periods where I thought it would be better for someone else to pitch hit for me, but I overcame all the stress and frustration that goes with making every dollar and penny count for something and weathered it pretty good. I have learned a lot about what to do and not to do and am in the process of changing my spending habits. I would be the first to admit I am not where I want to be when it comes to managing my money, but I am doing much better than I was doing a year ago. This is the puddle before me now. I need to resist the urge to turn it into a stormy sea, and allow Jesus to say, "Peace, be still."

Being an artist, I have difficulties not to be critical. I look at being critical as different from being judgmental. When people are critical, they understand how all the elements of a thing work to create a thing of beauty or ugliness. When people are judgmental, they are saying the person, place, or thing is good or evil and deserve heaven or hell; there is finality to their view on what they are judging. A critic describes a work of art, whereas a judge seeks to reward or diminish a work of art and place it in the scheme of other works of art.

Earlier I said that it is difficult for me to control love because it has so many different ways it can manifests itself. Whatever love can be, it is not judgmental. It's experiential and critical to the point of making that which is being critiqued better or the best it can be. My parents were and have been critical toward me as both a child and an adult. I don't always agree with them, but I know they love me. I am critical of other Christians because they don't live as I see Jesus lived, but then again our views of Jesus are probably different. I know a number of nonbelievers who live more like Jesus and walk his walk than those who say they do.

Judgment day is coming, if you believe in that event, but I don't think on that day God will judge us as some of the preachers declare it. Instead he will ask us to judge ourselves. "How have you treated the least of these?" he will ask us. "Have you looked at your fellow man and judged him unworthy of your love or have you seen a brother in the water drowning and reached out to keeping him from going under? Have you stirred up the water into a tempest causing the boat to capsize or have you spoken these words: 'Peace, be still.'"

If I am under a curse, so be it, I do not fear it, for God won't allow me to be tempted more than I am capable of resisting and tormented more than I can bear. The failings of my mind might manifest themselves again in my life, but hopefully, I will hold on to the hand of Jesus, for he will keep me from sinking into despair. This is my prayer.

My mind creates delusions as a way of preserving my sense of reality and peace. It makes a mental world in which I can exist without being frustrated by life's realities. However, it is a fragile bubble that bursts when poked. My mind under stress seeks the path of least resistance, so it continues to create bubbles over and over again. I have come to think of it as similar to my immune system. Sometimes it is in balance, and other times it is out of balance. I have to constantly check it, like I check my blood glucose levels every day for my diabetes. It requires a constant vigilance to make sure it is not over- or underproducing imaginary worlds, which is my sanctuary from the stresses that can create another psychotic episode.

HAPPINESS

18 April

If you had asked me six months or two weeks ago if I could be happy, I would have said no without hesitation. Today, however, the sun is shining, a light breeze is coming out of the northwest, the grass is green and freshly cut, and it is moderately warm. A picture-perfect, beautiful day, and yes, I am happy. I can count on one hand the number of times I have been this happy in the last twenty-six years. However, happiness is a fragile, and often fleeting, state of mind.

Today my parents picked me up for supper. They were taking me out to celebrate my birthday. I got in the car, and within five minutes, there was tension in the air. My mother asked me if I had gotten permission to use the names of the people I referred to in the book. I tried to explain that it is written in a diary format and style, so that I might tell my story from my perspective. She wouldn't hear my case for the diary. All she could think about is that someone was going to sue me. Her words stabbed me in the heart. I don't know all that was in her mind, but anything I tried to say she didn't want to hear, because she didn't want to argue about it. I was ready to ask my dad to take me back home. This wasn't going to be a good time together; I could feel it. But I resisted my impulses, and in time the sun did come out again. Our meal together turned out rather well. I even had the opportunity to share why I was writing the diary and my intent.

When I told them that I had written an entry in my diary stating that, while I could not declare myself a Christian, I could say that I was a follower of Christ, the ice under our feet seemed to melt. We even talked about the members of our family who had the same mental health issues as I. Our conversation relaxed and turned toward the better. I told them that writing was the only way I knew how to express what was on my mind and in my heart and that God gave me these gifts and talents to use to help others like me. We connected.

My mom grew up under the strict discipline of her mother and with a father who was a peacemaker and whom as a girl she couldn't trust with things she wanted to talk about in confidence. There has always been tension between my mother and her mother who still lives in Florida. I told her that I had learned to hide what I was experiencing, feeling, and thinking because like her I didn't have anyone in my family that I could count on for support and speak to in confidence. This cycle needs to be broken. We need to talk about the pain and the shame that is being passed down from one generation to the next.

My mom expressed her feelings of guilt for passing on to me this genetic tendency for periods of mental illness. She had endured the pain of childbirth, and then to have a child who struggled with delusions and emotional instability was more then she could bear at times. She wanted the past to be the past and move on. I had to tell her I couldn't move on, for I always had to be on guard lest I slip back into another state of mental and emotional turmoil. There is no cure for the disorders, which is my cross to bear.

I don't wish on anyone what I have to deal with day in and day out. The fact remains that the creator has made me a fragile vessel that is easily broken. I can be repaired but will always be fragile. This doesn't mean I want people to feel they have to leave me alone or walk on tippy toes around me. I am that I am, a vessel that Jesus can use to turn water into wine.

Psychically and emotionally, the nerves of my being are close to the surface and often lying open on the surface. There is no thick hide of skin between me and those around me. I feel things differently and more intensely than most. This is the way I am.

By the Pool
Oil, 24 × 36 inches
1997

The painting above, titled *By the Pool,* is a self-portrait. The characters in the painting are members of my family, taken from individual sketches and photographs of each of them doing something in or out of the pool over the course of a summer in the late 1980s. I am the only one not depicted in the scene; however, it is from my perspective looking on from a corner of the pool. A Jewish family that lives near Detroit, Michigan, purchased the painting from me. It has been the only Internet sale of my oil paintings thus far and is probably one of the best of my career. In the painting, I am providing a glimpse not just of my family but of myself as well. Each character is in his or her little world enjoying the benefits of the pool area but not really relating or interacting with the other characters. My relationship with my family is mixed. Like in any typical American family, there are dominant and submissive personalities. Each has a role to play in the overall family psyche

AVATAR

I watched the movie *Avatar* last night from a DVD that I didn't see it in the movie theater when it came out last year. The movie shots are fabulous. I hope they develop this movie into a series like they did the Star Wars movie series. The writers borrowed heavily from Native American folklore and spirituality. It's going to take several viewings of the movie to grasp all the subtle nuances of the story line.

I belong to those who think that this galaxy is too large for just us humans to be the only sensate life-form to exist in it. I think that many worlds have been seeded with life and that someday, when mankind eventually evolves technologically and mentally, we will travel to those worlds and become apart of the larger cosmic order and community. We are still too primitive to be able to accomplish that kind of feat. I think and feel that science fiction is just one way in which we are preparing ourselves for that day, by exploring the possibilities and scenarios of how our relationship with extraterrestial species might be.

The Star Trek movie series wasn't the first, but it introduced us to the idea of first contact with another race that was humanoid in appearance but quite different from us emotionally and intellectually, the Vulcans. The Stargate series introduced us to the Ancients, who, according to the story line, were a once advanced humanoid race that seeded the universe with their genome at less developed levels. The Ancients eventually evolved to a point where they could leave their bodies and exist as pure energy and light. This sounds a lot like God and the angels; the Ancients even have their counterpart, the Ori, or dark side of the force.

The Holy Bible is full of descriptions of super-race beings. According to the scriptures, early men slept with angels creating beings who were giants. And we all know the story of the Tower of Babel, where God in his frustration

73

with mankind decided that it would be best if mankind spoke different languages, preventing us from undertaking projects that would have us think we could master our world the same as God. Twice, God stepped into mankind's development to keep us from advancing too fast, once with the Flood and then again at the Tower of Babel. If the scriptures are accurate, the next time God will reveal himself and interfere with our lives is when Jesus returns to stop the great battle of Armageddon.

Science fiction has been one of the ways that I have used to cope with the voices I hear. Allowing myself to imagine that the voices are not human in origin but supernatural is one way that I have dealt with them. Other persons who hear voices engage the voices in a conversation, and this can manifest itself in different ways. I have argued with these voices and pleaded and prayed but usually ended up feeling worse than before. The only way that I have been able to successfully deal with the voices is through distraction techniques like watching TV, listening to music, surfing the Internet, or writing in my journal or letters to the editor. I used to be able to distract myself through reading, but lately reading has been less enjoyable and less helpful as a diversion.

It probably is not all that healthy for me, but I go out for a smoke. Actually, smoking is one of the most popular tactics of persons with mental disorders to cope with their hallucinations. It helps me to relax and provides me with an activity to do at the same time. I usually go out for a cigarette every half hour. That means I am about a two-pack-a-day smoker. I have tried stretching the time between cigarettes to forty-five minutes to an hour, and I can usually do it if I am working on the computer. I get up two to three times during the night, mostly because I am awoken by pain in my legs and feet, but as part of the event, I go outside for a smoke, even when it's below freezing. I have cut back on my smoking but am not ready to give it up entirely quite yet. I was smoking three packs a day after my second stay at the Marion VA hospital, but when the cost of cigarettes and taxes went up, I knew I had to moderate my habit. I really don't think our society should put so much effort into exterminating cigarette smokers. We are treated like criminals and second class citizens by the self-righteous nonsmokers. I actually use my smoke periods as times to pray. I have a neighbor whose wife has Alzheimer's disease. I pray for them when I am outside doing my thing. It's the one religious thing that I do daily.

Like about everything in our society and culture if it is profitable we do it. The craze to eradicate smoking has become a whole new industry the last generation. All have their solutions to getting smokers to quit their dirty habit, but it all comes with a price tag. If smoking is such a big deal and if it is something that the majority wants done away with, then I think it should be a not-for-profit enterprise. As long as it's a money-making enterprise, I would rather smoke than not. If I have to pay for something, it might as well be something I enjoy. And the solutions to not smoking don't have much appeal from my point of view. There, I have said my two cents' worth on the topic.

The Gathering
Oil, 14 × 28 inches
2003

The work above is pretty much straightforward. I saw this group of horses standing along a tree line when I was out one day doing my assigned work for *Goshen News*. I portrayed them in silhouette because I thought it best portrayed the Amish and their unpretentious way of life. It is also one of the ways that I perceive people around me, devoid of individualistic characteristics. What makes the horses unique is their posture.

TODAY IS FOREVER

24 April

In February 2010 I began studying a book on money management as part of my contract agreement with the debt management company I contracted with. The book is fairly easy to read. At times the author spends a little more time providing examples and scenarios that drag on and on and seem to go nowhere specific but only take up space on the page. I prefer to read books in which the writer gets to the point, providing enough detail to make a point, or describes something without getting to wordy.

One of the things I have to deal with is the difficulty in remembering names of people and even words that I want to say. I used to be good at remembering people before I burned my legs but since the seriously high blood pressure I experienced early on after my legs were burned I have a great deal of difficulty recalling names or words when I most need them in a conversation. The only exception to this inability is when the person, place, or thing had a significant, dramatic impact on my life.

My visual arts professor who oversaw my degree program in art education at Goshen College was one such person. His knowledge and skill in the visual arts really impressed upon me how integral the arts were to our daily lives. It was this that I sought to teach my own students, be they young or old. The professor used his home for his gifts and talents with ceramics and pottery in about every aspect. In the entranceway there was a cast-iron wood-burning stove that didn't touch the floor. It was suspended from the ceiling, connected by the flue pipe; and the stove itself was a large cast-iron ball. The counters in the home were ceramic tile, and the light covers were made from clay. Even the toilet he designed out of clay, but it was not like any ordinary toilet. It was fashioned after the older gravity toilets, with a separate holding tank on the wall behind the toilet. In the living room there were various pieces of furniture made from clay, like the coffee table, which was a large open bowl with a glass top.

In his teaching, the professor emphasized the four pillars of the visual arts: production, history, criticism, and aesthetics. When I taught art to elementary students, I made it a point of giving them a well-rounded approach to the visual arts. It wasn't just about creating a beautiful drawing or painting, but understanding how observation played a role in telling a story on a two-dimensional surface. I once had a discussion about the curriculum with the assistant superintendent of the school system. He told me that he wanted art to be fun for the students. I disagreed with him. I didn't want art to be just fun, an easy grade, but something that gave meaning to their lives. After I left that school system, I had conversations with the art teachers in the upper grades of that school system, and they all said my students were the best-prepared, most knowledgeable about the visual arts as any they had ever had. One of my elementary art students later went on to study art education for her degree in college, so I feel some sense of pride that my efforts were not in vain.

I think and feel what we do today is forever; however, that is not enough. Teaching reading, writing, and math is not enough if we want to be ready for tomorrow. Tomorrow's decision makers and doers must be able to think and feel that what they do makes a difference. Our current education system too heavily emphasizes learning rote or doing well on the tests. I don't see life as one test after another but as a series of experiences constantly engaging us in assessing, producing, recording, and defining our existence. Tomorrow's workers must be able to analyze a problem before they can solve a problem. They must know it forward and backward. Too much of the time, we just deal with the surface of an issue without getting at the root cause.

When I was in middle school, one of my favorite noon time activities was playing chess. I am not much of chess player today, but one of the lessons I learned from that game was you need to think several moves ahead of the move you are playing. That's the way you win. The best chess players and masters of the game have the game well in hand even before they make the first move. When I taught art, I thought of my students as adults in the making. They were blank slates and sponges. I didn't talk to them as children but as individuals who could comprehend complex things if only given the right preparation and leading. I understood where my students were developmentally, but that was only the starting point. I envisioned where they would be after the instruction I gave them.

In the title of this diary, I refer to myself as a delusional man. In many ways I do think delusionally, but in other ways I think with clarity. A neighbor that I had over for supper last night said that we should allow geniuses that are insane remain insane if what they can provide us is more than what they could provide being sane. Too often we focus on curing a thing when we would do better allowing it to take its course and benefit from what it can offer us. I don't think we should allow a madman invent something that could kill hundreds or thousands of people. We have to exercise common sense. I am glad for the treatment I have received from the VA and others. It has helped me understand what I am dealing with and what others are dealing with when they relate to me. I don't want to be of harm to another person or myself, and when that occurs, intervention is totally appropriate. Yet, if we nullify the energy of a person who does not think like normal people do, then we do a great disservice to ourselves and our children who might benefit from harnessing that energy.

It all comes down to managing the mind's state. Right now I think and feel that my medications are working to my benefit. I don't feel lethargic or out of it. I am able to make decisions based on facts and evidence that are rooted in reality. I still experience periods of anxiousness, but I am not debilitated by the emotions that sweep over me when I feel that way. I have learned ways of coping, such as taking a nap for fifteen minutes or more, or going outside to have a smoke, maybe two if I need to. I even know I cannot deal with everything in my life, and in certain situations I have to allow others to deal with the problem or issue and trust they are doing what is best for me. That doesn't mean I want to become totally dependent on others. I need to have a balance where I put together a reasonable amount of effort to accomplishing a task, solving a problem, or creating something new. Take away those things that give people purpose and meaning, and they will soon be nothing worth living.

If we remember that today is forever, however long that is, then we are on the right path. It is the journey down that path, wherever it may take us, that is what life is all about.

WE ARE THAT WE ARE

25 April

This afternoon I watched the 1966 futuristic movie *Fahrenheit 451*. It's about a possible period of time when books are banned, in fact when society rejects anything written. It's pretty advanced for the '60s. There are even wide-screen TVs, and instead of calling each other comrades, people are referred to as cousins. The only backward element in the movie is the old-style phones. The main character in the movie is Montag, a "fireman," whose job is not to put out fires but burn books. The station house where he works is called Firehouse 451, which is the temperature at which book paper ignites and burns. Montag meets a young woman and, through the development of their relationship, he learns that she reads books that she and others have hidden. Montag begins taking a book here and there and hides them in his home. Then he gets up during the night and reads them. Montag's wife discovers him reading one night and eventually turns him in.

The movie reminds me of the movement in the 1980s and '90s to ban certain books that were thought to be to perverted or unsuitable for public reading. It was led by those who called themselves conservatives, the Moral Majority. When I was young, it was easy for me to get caught up in extreme or radical ways of thinking and acting. Politically, I have trouble with the Republicans and the planks of that party. Conservatism is also something I have trouble swallowing. I know a number of conservatives who are good caring people and who I am happy to call my friends. I don't consider myself a liberal or even a moderate. What I can't stomach is all the political crybabies, who only whine and do nothing to really solve the problems that our society and culture are facing.

It makes me sad that in our culture and society a big thing is made about what a person is or is not. I think politically we should get rid of the two-party system and require all candidates for public office go through the same process as anyone seeking a job. They should provide a résumé or credentials stating how they are qualified for the position they are seeking. Anyone should be able to apply for a position in government as long as they had a certain number of signatures from the people they want to represent and the right credentials.

What persons seeking office would need to prove is that they had the skills and knowledge to carry out the work of governing at whatever level of government they were seeking to work at. They would need to know the laws and regulations that were related to the job they wanted to hold office in. If they sought a government position in the national government, such as congressman or senator, they would need to know and understand state laws as well as international law, because they would be called upon to vote on treaties with other countries. All office seekers would need to be excellent communicators and able to work with men and women who had different views and perspectives on what was right or wrong for this country.

Those elected to office would hold that position for a predetermined time period. When their time was done they would be assigned to teach government courses at a college or university, thus preparing the next generation for the jobs they might aspire to.

My thoughts on what government should be might be an ideal and part of a delusion, but I think and feel it's a better way than what we currently have. The persons elected to office may take positions on specific issues that their government offices are responsible for, but that wouldn't be party positions. Political parties would not be allowed, and there would be no party minority whip or majority whip to corral its members in voting as a block on certain bills, regulations, or laws.

The federal judiciary would go through the same election process as all other persons seeking to serve in public office. No more would they be appointed by one person and affirmed by a specific body of elected officials. In this way their allegiance would not be to the left or right but to all constitutes. They would be chosen for their insight of law and wisdom. They to would be elected for an allotted time period and then assigned to a teaching job after they completed their term.

Little Boy Blue
Oil, 18 × 24 inches
2002

FLASHBACKS

26 April

I woke up several times last night in pain. I also had nightmares of being on fire. The sheets were soaking wet. I was tossing and turning in my bed but eventually fell asleep on the couch. When I finally got up, I was exhausted. I don't have the dreams as often as I did when I was first discharged from the army hospital twenty-six years ago, but they do come from time to time. My legs and feet are still sore today, and the pain meds are having only marginal effect in reducing the pain. I still have to get up from sitting on the couch or office chair every thirty minutes or so. There's little I can do about the pain; I just have to try and refocus my attention on something else and hope the distraction will be enough.

The problem with having to deal with the pain is it triggers flashbacks, even during the day. Most of the time the flashbacks don't make much sense, but I get a mixture of emotions from them, such as anger, despair, frustration, sadness, and so forth.

A thought that I still struggle with to this day is *Could I take another's life?* I trained with a variety of weapons in the army when I was a sharpshooter with the M16 rifle and M60 machine gun. When I enlisted in the artillery, I thought I would be back from the front lines and would not have to deal much with the enemy face-to-face unless they infiltrated our lines. I guess I was prepared to kill a human being in case of a mortal threat to my comrades. I knew I was ready to give up my life if that had been required of me. I wasn't afraid to die. What haunted me though was taking innocent life, the life of civilians. When they trained us to use nuclear weapons for tactical purpose, I began having nightmares about women and children maimed and killed. I could not justify what I was doing anymore, and my gut got all twisted.

My superiors often asked me the question, "What would you do if someone broke into your home and threatened your wife and children? Would you use deadly force to protect them?" When they asked that question, I thought of my Amish ancestors who lived in Germantown, Pennsylvania, in the 1700s and were attacked one evening by a band of Indians. The only survivors were my great-great-great-great-grandfather and two of his sons. I wondered how they felt after seeing the rest of their family butchered by those Indians. They survived, and I am their descendant. *Were they cowards? How much rage would it take for me to kill other human beings? Could I do it dispassionately? They*

82

are the enemy, and my job was to destroy the enemy. Was that God's will? If the enemy killed me, was that God's will too? When I began thinking these types of thoughts and had these types of questions that I could not answer, my mind began to spin in all kinds of directions, and I hated myself.

I thought about my place in the military and the Cold War conflict that we faced as soldiers. They told us we were mainly there as a deterrent, to make the enemy, the East Germans and Russians, think twice before taking hostile actions. Why did we hate each other so much that we had to constantly threaten the other side? Was there a right and a wrong side? What did the Soviets think of us? Could we ever have been friends?

The questions just kept on coming, and I saw no resolution that I could believe in. I just knew that I didn't want to take the life of innocent civilians by using a nuclear round simply to stop one or two Soviet tanks. I didn't think it was right, even if it was a weapon of last resort. When I asked my senior officers these questions, their responses didn't satisfy me. I was beginning to feel that Dexter was right: I had chosen God's plan B for my life. I wanted a way out, so I would never have to be forced to be involved in using a nuclear weapon on anyone. It was insane, mad. I began questioning my own sanity for being part of this conflict. I struggled with thoughts of harming myself or doing something that would get me thrown out of the army. But of everything I thought of, I knew it was a nonanswer. I felt trapped and could not move.

When I went AWOL on June 21, 1983, I did so with the intent of getting psychiatric help. I knew my mind wasn't right, and needed to find someone I could trust. I wasn't sure that I could trust the psychiatrists at the army hospital, but I knew I couldn't trust my commanders. I needed a solution that would allow me to finish my tour, but not as a combatant soldier. Every part of my being hurt, and I needed some relief; just a sliver of hope was all I wanted.

I painted the oil painting titled *Targeting It* after I got out of the VA hospital in 2004. It was one of the final four paintings of a series of eight that I did between December 2003 and August 2004. I did not feel as inspired or passionate about the last four paintings as I had about the first four. That was due in part because of the medication they had me on. My emotions were muted from the dosage of drugs I was taking. But I knew the series was incomplete, so I forced myself to paint. This painting dealt with my mental and emotional struggle in West Germany where I was stationed. I was seeking a balance, a compromise between the light and dark forces that were in my head. The two mannequin figures represent how I felt. One part of me wanted to be a fighting soldier, a leader of men. The other part of me wanted to surrender. I felt like I had ignited a fuse that was going to lead to my own destruction mentally and spiritually. I explored various combinations of color and texture and brushwork. I saw my psychological state as interlocking and curvilinear, which is also representsative of the dynamics of my emotional state.

THE HEARING

28 April

Today was my personal hearing at the Indianapolis VA Regional Office. It wasn't what I had imagined it to be. There was only one person representing the VA, and then there were my Disabled American Veterans representative, who spoke on my behalf; my father, who gave testimony; and I. The hearing lasted twelve minutes, and now I will have to wait for them to send the digital recording to California, where it will be transcribed, and then sent back to Indianapolis, where the full committee will weigh the evidence and facts pertaining to my proposed incompetency declaration. It could easily take months before I hear anything. The VA and DAV representatives thought I made a good defense against being declared incompetent, but I am basically at the mercy of those who will make the final decision. They told me to not fret over it, just be patient.

I am basically at peace about whatever decision the VA makes with regard to my state of competency, even though I would rather they did not declare me incompetent. However, looking at my life and impulsive decisions, they would be fully justified in declaring me so. Our Declaration of Independence states that we have "Life, Liberty and the pursuit of Happiness." But does that mean that we have the right to make decisions that would harm ourselves or others? That is the question. Am I harming myself or others when I make impulsive or irrational decisions? Some would think so.

Impulsiveness is in my nature. I try to resist the urge to make spur-of-the-moment decisions; however, I am not always successful. It's not that I can't resist the temptation, because more often then not, I do manage to put on hold making a decision to purchase a thing or do something that I feel like doing. The problem that I face is sometimes I am unable to think about how a decision will affect me in the long term. I lack the ability to see beyond the moment, the now. I am a risk taker. I rationalize the taking of risks by thinking that nothing will get done unless I take a risk and do something. It's not hard for me to see the possibility of doing something and the outcome that would result if I only took the risk. People take risks everyday. Some turn out for the good, and some for the not so good. Some people are lucky, and some people are not so lucky. It's a crapshoot at best.

THE PRINCIPLE OF A THING

2 May

From 1996 to 2000, I worked in five different jobs. They never amounted to anything significant. I felt strongly that, if I was to be a good husband and father, I should take the lead and provide for my family. I had the benefits that my disability with the VA provided, but I didn't want to be a charity case. I was raised with the principle that you work by the sweat of your brow. This principle drove me to seek out jobs that enabled me to earn a living for my family and that were needed by the community I was part of.

However, all those jobs seemed to come to a point where I was in conflict with someone on the job, be it a boss or other employee, over some principle that I felt was too important. Once I was a safety and compliance officer for a transportation company. When I first went to work at the company, I was a temp hired to do data entry. The businesses computer system had crashed, and they lost a year worth of data because the backup system also failed. It was to be a two-week assignment, but I was able to complete it in four days. The boss was so impressed with my work ethic, and another employee was leaving, that I was offered the job. It wasn't something that I had been trained for, but I felt confident that I could fairly quickly pick up the skills and knowledge needed. What I didn't learn in the interview until several months later was the boss was hired by the family that owned the company to be a hatchet man. While I was there, many employees that were good workers and long-time employees were fired, which made for a turbulent work environment. I finally reached a point where I could no longer be an instrument of a man who was able to terminate whoever he wanted, anytime he wanted. Not long after I quit, I learned that he too was fired by the owners of the company.

During this period of my life, I also went through several bouts of depression. The stress at work and at home compounded a sense of failure and low self-esteem. I sought out professionals for help, but what these therapy sessions offered me was simply an ill-fitting Band-Aid. The church offered me even less, and I grew to hate God. The feelings of isolation increased. Dread consumed my thoughts and heart. I thought of ending my life, but the stigma that went with committing suicide prevented me from dwelling on it. The sense of loss of control spun me in a downward spiral. I would go months between jobs unable to do anything except eat and sleep.

My wife often told me I should just focus on my art, but I was so fixated on finding the right job that I couldn't get inspired to spend hours on end doing something that no one would buy. I knew that the kind of art I had done would not have been appreciated in my community, and I had no marketing skills or no one to represent me where my art would have been valued. I considered doing the kind of crafty art production work that could sell cheaply and easily, but it was the principle of the thing that prevented me from committing myself to it.

GRACE OF GOD

4 May

I met with my VA social worker today, and she asked me, "How do you get back up? What is it that causes you to go on even though you have been knocked down so many times?"

Jesus said, "I am the way, the truth, and the life. No man comes to the Father but through me." I feel and think that God has a purpose for my life and that I am living it. I am far from perfect, but even in me his hand is at work perfecting me. At times I succumb to darkness. It overwhelms me and I fall, but God in his love reaches out and picks me up. That is the only way I know how to describe it. I have experienced God's love over and over and over again. He has not given up on me and never will. He has made me as I am—a testament of his enduring love. Because of this love, I have hope and because of this hope, he begets his faith to and through me. If I have faith, it is in Jesus, not the many religions that men have constructed in his name. I am that I am because Jesus takes me to the Father and shows me the light.

My art is my way of revealing what I have learned because of Jesus's work in me. He is my muse. My art has not won acclaim and that is okay because I did not create it for my glory. I created it for God, for he is my inspiration.

Father's Hands
Oil, 18 × 24 inches
1993

    This painting depicts my father holding my cousin's daughter, Megan, when she was around three years old. It's a warm summer day around the pool side. My father holds and protects her from scurrying off and hurting herself. Eventually, he will take her into the cool water of the pool, but she is content for now to be held by my father.

    I gave this painting to Megan after her father, my cousin Greg, was killed by a deranged worker in the plant he managed in Goshen. I don't know the status of this painting; all I have is a photocopy of the painting. I wanted to comfort her in the loss of her father.

    I have a lot of sadness from the gulf that has come between me and my family. Yet I too know that God has a purpose for this state of being, if even only to draw me closer to him. He has not taken from me my memories of a loving family, which I learned a great deal and received much from. Still, in my solitude I am more aware of my heavenly Father and his work in me. This diary is part of that work.

Every day I am reminded that God doesn't give up; he is steadfast. The way of the world is to create religions. Their founders were well-meaning and many were men of God, but we cannot come to the Father through them, but only through Jesus.

My mother told me after I was discharged from Brooke Army Medical Center back in 1983, that I have always lived outside the walls of the family. She probably spoke the truth. I am in a way a wanderer I have never felt safe or content being part of my earthly family. It's not that I don't love them and care about them; it's just that I feel called to live in my own space, where I can hear God's voice. Unfortunately, I hear other voices too. In a crowd or social gathering I feel uncomfortable. It's not natural for me. I am not a social creature. There were times that I wondered if I was adopted. Except for my facial features, I am unlike anyone in my family. I often felt like I was the black sheep of the family.

A lot of people in our area know my parents, brother, and sister, but they are often surprised at meeting me because they don't know I am related to them I don't feel or think that I am better than them, just different. I am actually happy and proud of their accomplishments and in some ways jealous. I wish at times that I was more like them. But if I am to follow Jesus, I need to put aside my earthly ties and walk the path he has set before me. It's a path that only I can walk if I am to know him. All children of God have their own path on which they have to follow Jesus. It's are not the same for everyone.

When I wander off the path, I find myself overcome by darkness, and that's when the voices have their way with me. They are always calling me to leave the path, and many times I have followed these voices. But as the psalmist wrote, "thy rod and thy staff, they comfort me." When I am overcome with emotions, he comes to me and holds me in his hands.

DADA

5 May

Historically, the visual arts had three primary purposes: decorative, political, and spiritual-religious. During the early 1900s, the arts took on new meanings. One of these movements produced one of my favorite artists, Marcel Duchamp. He was part of a group of artists who referred to their creations as *Dada*. The group of artists was about creating anti-war and anti-art cultural works. They often gathered to discuss art, politics, and culture. The movement began in Zurich, Switzerland, during World War I. The group influenced other avant-garde movements, such as surrealism, *Nouveau Réalisme*, pop art, *Fluxus*, and punk rock. It was also influential in creating the groundwork for abstract art and sound poetry.

Marcel Duchamp came up with a type of art he called *readymades*. He took a urinal, set it on its back, signed it "R. Mutt," and titled it *Fountain*. Another one of his readymades was a postcard of the *Mona Lisa* which he drew a mustache and goatee on. He was also a master chess player and often spent hours strategizing intricate chess moves.

My art is done in two different styles: realism and abstract realism. I draw from the impressionist love of color; my paintings are brightly colored. The boldness of color is indicative of my emotional state upon observing subject matter that I think and feel would make a good composition for what I want to express. My paintings are both hot and cold, signifying my spiritual being at different times during a manic-depressive episode.

In my Crete series, I depict sights that I observed while touring the island during a two-week international artist workshop, sponsored by a local gallery in Chania, Crete. The gallery, Omma, has since gone out of business. The paintings are about the local color and architecture. Common subject matter and themes in the paintings are doorways and cats. The Greek people love cats; they can be found everywhere on the island. I came up with the subject matter for the paintings from sketches and photographs that I took while walking the streets and byways. It was a place that I fell in love with, for there is a lot of pride in the people of Crete.

There are seldom any people in my paintings, except for my early paintings and the abstract series I did between 2004 and 2006. In the abstract paintings, I incorporated mannequins that I posed for the renderings. Some of my early paintings are figurative. I did those paintings to demonstrate a mastery of the human form. They are technically sound but lack the emotion that my later works contain.

Each of my paintings represents a world unto itself, a place in my mind that I can go to and rest. In that place I process the stresses, moods, emotions, and rational or irrational thoughts of the day or week. Each choice of color, brushstroke, and mark reflects my attempt to make real the imagery of my mind.

Ice-Cream Maidens
Oil, 24 × 36 inches
2002

One of the common techniques I use in creating paintings is the merging of multiple photos. In this painting, I used five different photos. The Amish girls were actually on a photo taken at a local school, and the backdrop was a brick wall. I have always admired the impressionist painters, and while my paintings are more realistic in style, I borrow their use of pure pigments and bright hues in my paintings. The flow of contour lines creates the illusion of movement, carrying the viewer's eyes in and around the painting. I genuinely appreciate the simplicity of the Amish lifestyle. Their hard work and simple pleasures have always been something that I have tried to emulate in my life. While I am still very English, as they refer to those not of their faith, doctrinally the core of their relationship with the world and others has significantly influenced me.

MONKEY BARS

11 December

The last week I felt depressed; I think it is the holidays. My relationships with friends and family have either been intense or distant. Lately, it has been a feeling of distrust. I have been hurt so many times. When I got close to those I believed I could connect, I always found out that my faith in them had been betrayed. I am at a point now, in my early fifties, that I am not sure I can start over again with someone else.

I know I need human contact. The question is *Can I overcome my own history with others?* Is it possible for someone like me who in the past has been so self-destructive to find someone whom I can coexist with?—someone whom I can confide in with total confidence. This I do with my social worker and a few others within the VA system, but these relationships are official in nature.

Living in a self-made world of imagination has been the norm for my life. Animals know the boundaries of their place in their habitat. The monkeys are social, and at the same time solitary, creatures. They forage for food and attend to each other by grooming. They play and mate and spend hours silently sitting on the perch of their kingdom. Sometimes I see myself as a monkey.

The scriptures tell us that God cares for the smallest creature, that one doesn't fall without his knowledge. He provides for their needs. Of course animals don't require clothing and many go without any shelter from the extreme elements because our Father in heaven has made them with skins that protect them in the environment they are designed to live in. Compared to animals, humans are by far the minority, yet we do the most damage to our habitat. Why is that?

By far the majority of animals don't waste or want. Their life span may be brief or lengthy. It may be one of peace or danger. They live their lives as some part of the food chain, yet you don't hear them complain about their lot in life. They are born accepting what life has to offer them.

Among humanity there are some who live to love the creatures they coexist with. There are others who feel threatened by all or a few of the animals, which God has made and to which we are given stewardship responsibilities. In the new earth and heaven, the God of us all will make the lion lay down with the lamb. There is even an insurance company television ad that exploits this idea.

We live in a world today that is exponentially being consumed by technology. More and more, we can connect with others through cell phones, iPods, webcams, and chat rooms. Still, I wonder if we really see our fellow men and their true spirits. How deep do we go in our connection with others? With many persons I have exposed myself too cognitively and spiritually, only to find out that they were offended by my sins and didn't see the grace of God at work in me. Is it that I don't know how to communicate this to them? I can relate to Moses who didn't think and feel he was God's man to deliver his people from bondage.

Jesus was only understood by a handful of people that he ministered to. His words were not received; the language that he spoke was foreign to those he spoke to. He preformed miracles and did many things that should have made the majority of those he testified to acknowledge him as the son of man and son of God. Still, he sat alone surrounded by the masses.

Oh What a Chump I Am
Pen and ink, 9 × 12 inches
1998

Many of the artworks I have created represent the solitude of my life. While distinctly a social creature, I have preferred being by myself. It has always seemed that when I get close to others, things don't turn out the way I would desire or hope. I only know that God's purpose and will is always at work.

DESIRE TO BE NORMAL

9 May

Today I am calmer than yesterday. I feel like I have more energy than I did twenty-four hours ago. It's amazing how one day can make a difference. My body chemistry shifts for no apparent reason. I am eating healthier than I have in months, so it's not what I am eating that's causing these chemical shifts. I am having regular bowel movements. The only difference between yesterday and today is yesterday I only had one cup of coffee instead of my usual ten. Coffee is a stimulant, but for some reason, it has the opposite effect on me and settles my mood.

I have known other people who were bipolar and who had to watch what they ate because the wrong foods caused them to go through manic-depressive episodes. My diet is more for my diabetes than anything else. The medication that I take for my diabetes goes a long way at keeping my blood glucose levels in the normal range. I can eat pretty much anything I want, but I have to watch the amount of sugar I take in because I get light-headed when I overdo it.

I made an impulse purchase yesterday on eBay. I bid on one item and won the bid at seventy-five dollars. I knew it was a mistake almost immediately after I made it. I requested that the bid be nullified. Fortunately, my request was accepted, and I got my money back.

I am seriously thinking about quitting smoking. I may be forced to do so this month because I don't have the money to spend on cigarettes. We will see how it goes.

My cell phone and cable bills were higher than in the past months and have depleted my reserve cash that I usually have. I have just enough to pay for the groceries.

I let some of my meds run down to the bare minimum before reordering. I will have to do without until I get the refills. I am taking a chance doing so, but I think I can manage for three or four days. My legs and feet have been causing me more pain than normal the last week or so. I have an appointment coming up with my VA primary care physician. I think and feel like my body is adapting to the pain meds they have me on. They say the next time they change my pain meds, they will put me on a longer-lasting kind that is time-released.

My VA therapist asked me three days ago if I was having any manic-depressive tendencies. I lied by saying no. I have been having strong urges to do irrational things. The impulse purchase of the TV on Ebay was a minor instance. Lying is also something that is characteristic of persons who are bipolar. If we told the truth all the time about how we feel all the time, we would be shackled and locked up and the key thrown away.

I don't get any pleasure from telling a lie, but I don't want people to think I am always negative. I do have many things to be thankful for, and want people to have a positive image of the person I am. The problem is that who I am and how I feel don't always mesh. There are things in my life that I have no control over and that I am often overwhelmed by. Even if it's for a day or so, I would like to know what it is like to be normal.

SOCIAL CREATURES

11 May

I watched the *X-Men* series movies on FX this afternoon. The last movie in the series *X-Men: The Last Stand* reminded me of my own mutant condition and the struggle within me. On the one hand, when I am manic or schizoaffective, my mental state is heightened. I am aware of more things, and my emotions while raw make me feel superior to normal's. On the other hand, they don't when I am depressed, and the voices disrupt the quiet and calmness that I was feeling. I would accept anything that could permanently cure me. However, there is no cure yet. Being alone has its advantages and disadvantages. I am not swayed by the group swings from one extreme to another, but I do miss the friendship that comes with being a member of a group, a social structure.

Mooers at Work
Pen and ink, 9 × 12 inches
1998

In the pen-and-ink drawing titled *Mooers at Work*, I explore the activity of social creatures. Cows serve two purposes: keeping the grass down and producing milk. They also give birth to calves that become milk cows, bulls, or beef cattle. Social creatures usually live in some type of contained area where they dwell, live, and operate. A solitary creature, such as myself, is not contained to one space, unless locked.

When I am admitted to the acute care ward at the Marion VA hospital, initially I appreciate being contained in a safe place, but the wondering and trapped feelings eventually come out, and all I can think of is when am I going to be discharged. I often thought that I would like to join a monastery, where the basic needs are provided and I wouldn't have to worry about money. I could work on my art and do whatever assignments they required of me. But God has not led me in that direction so far; maybe someday.

I have often thought of joining the Catholic Church for that reason. When I was a young adult, I looked for social groups in which I could be free to do what I was called to do, yet have my basic needs provided. The Mennonite Church and the army provided that for a time, but I found myself needing to wander and exist in my own space. I couldn't conform to the discipline of a social or military structure.

The Tourist is a portrait of my brother in the Dominican Republic helping out a local farmer plow his field. My brother is a social creature and makes friends fairly readily. He has the ability to gather round him people of all types. He's a leader. I have never felt comfortable doing what he does so naturally. He follows the path of least resistance in almost everything he does. I, on the contrary, find myself in conflict with almost everyone I have ever known at some time or another.

12 May

Past Cathedral
Oil, 18 × 24 inches
2003

This painting represents my thoughts on the construction of church buildings by various religious groups. When I first attended Dexter's church, they were using a Christian high school for their gatherings. During the week, they met in the homes of elders and deacons of the church body. I thought this was innovative of them and closely resembled the Amish, who meet in each other's homes to hold their worship services. I feel and think that the construction of massive structures to worship is a waste of energy and money. Early believers didn't construct houses of worship like they do today. They were content to meet in existing places, be they homes, catacombs, hillsides, or whatever served their needs. Christians didn't start building edifices for worship until the Roman Empire officially recognized Christianity as a religion and stopped persecuting believers. Then they became more formal in almost every way. They lost their way. Dexter's church lost its way when they decided to build a structure for their worship services and other activities. For some odd reason, Christians and followers of other religions feel the need to make a statement that they are legitimate once they have an official place of worship.

I much prefer to worship in an old barn or home than in a wondrously designed piece of architecture. God can be in any place, but I feel closest to him where mammon is a less dominant motivator for the place to come close to him.

Biking Through Paradise
Oil, 18 × 24 inches
2002

Biking Through Paradise was my attempt to copy a painting and incorporate my own elements to make it mine. In this case, the bicyclists were added to give the painting additional meaning. The two figures are struggling upward in a beautiful scenery. This is their place of worship. I think and feel that worship does not need be singing, praying, or preaching but living and having fun in a place where you can almost touch God or his divine nature.

TENDER MERCIES

14 May

Last night was rough; I woke up twice because my legs felt like they were on fire. I dreamt that I was wandering endless hallways with doors on either side, and in the rooms were burn victims screaming in pain and agony. This went on and on until I woke up in a sweat. I had to change pillows because they were so wet. I heard those voices, "Burn yourself before they burn you." The dream is a common one. They become more frequent around the anniversary of the event back in 1983. The emotion is so deep that even the medication the VA has me on cannot minimize it, especially at night when I am unconscious. When I dream like that, my days seem to go on forever. I am tired and agitated during the day. I try to refocus and tell myself that it's only a memory, but I feel like it could happen all over again.

I know I am forgiven, yet I pray for peace and mercy. I want to run, but I can't, and I have nowhere to go. It takes all my mental will power to refocus my mind on other things. I think about my children and what outstanding adults they have become. I must have done something right for them to turn out the way they have. I think about the art lessons and students I have taught art and about the fun we had learning about the visual arts and its practical application in our daily lives. I try to shut out those memories of jobs I failed at and think about the fact that I did work when I was able. However, I want my time now to count for something more than just me. I want my life to be an inspiration to others who suffer in a similar way.

Thanking the divine for continuing to believe in me and walk with me through the dark periods of my life is the only thing that keeps me from falling off the deep end of life. There is no complicated thought process and mental exercise that one must do to push back the negative emotions that sweep over someone like me. It's a simple formula that anyone can do, yet you still have to work at it with your entire mind, heart, and spirit. When you fall, you simply have to get up and continue on the path of gratitude knowing it is not you who lights your path but Jesus. You only need to stay close to him, and you will see the way you are to go.

Thinking about others that fare worse than you is also something you need to focus on. I think about people who labor all day for a scrap of food and who do not have the niceties of life that I have. What can I do to make their lives easier and richer? Good works will not get you in the good graces of the Father, but we are called to serve our fellow men.

I have tried to volunteer through various agencies, but I have been rejected because of my history of mental illness and my attempted suicide. I have to find other ways to give, but time and my knowledge of life are the only spare things I have worth anything. I wish people wouldn't see me for what I have done but for what I am capable of doing and being. I know the tender mercies of the Father, Son, and Spirit; these I could share plenty of with those who need that sort of thing in their lives.

ON A SOAPBOX

Since my attempted suicide last September, love has been one of the hardest things for me to get my head around. When I was in the acute care ward of the Marion VA hospital, my parents sent me a box of clothes that I needed. I had been sent down to the hospital with only the clothes that I wore that day. In the box they put a book and a brief note. My mom said that she did not know how to help me but that she still loved me. I became angry when I read that note. No one from my family called or visited me when I was in the hospital. I felt totally isolated, cut-off from the ones I counted on for support and love. In reply to my mother's note, I wrote a two-page letter in which I said, "Saying you love me is not enough." I wanted more than just the words *I love you*.

We say *I love you* so often that it loses its meaning. It becomes something frivolous. When I was nine or ten years old, I memorized three hundred Bible verses one year so that I could go to the church camp one summer for free. Many of those verses I have forgotten, but one verse remains because it is probably the most important words ever spoken. The verse is John 3:16, "For God so loved the world, that he gave his only begotten Son, that whosoever believeth on him should not perish, but have eternal life." When I was a child, I really didn't know what that meant. It sounded good, but what did it mean for God to give us his only son?

When my mother said that she loved me, what did she mean? Is a mother's love enough to see you through the darkest moments in your life? We can survive for a while without food or water, but can we survive without God's love? No, we are damned to everlasting torment separated from God's love. I understand torment all too well. I need more than spoken words to survive; I need to believe in Jesus.

How do I show God my love? The answer I have already stated: faith in Jesus. To believe that he is enough to help me overcome my sinful tendency to fail utterly when I try to do well, I need to have faith in him even when darkness overwhelms me. That is how I show God that I love him. It's not enough to say *I love God*; I must be willing to give up everything that I cherish in this life. I must endure the sorrow of loss and despair so that I might not regain that which I once possessed.

God gave us his son. What did God give up to show us his love? He put his son on the line between life and death. He believed in his son enough that he was willing to sacrifice him for our sins. Some may say that God didn't really sacrifice anything at all, because he knew beforehand that his son would succeed in overcoming death. He knew that he would get him back. Did he really? Or did God take a chance and risk everything without knowing for sure that Jesus would live up to all that had been prophesied about him?

Yahweh made a lot of grand statements about his son's salvation for the world before he ever came to earth. If God knew for certain that his son would live up to his promise to us, than he really didn't sacrifice anything at all. I think God had faith in his son, but he was blind to the end result; he had to take a chance and risk everything. Saying that might not sit well with the predestination crowd, but that is what I think and feel. All God asks of us is that we too believe in his son and believe that what he did on Calvary was enough to enable us to live life everlasting.

Faith is not an easy thing. We are driven by our senses, and that is why we are sinners. The faith of Yahweh is more than flesh and blood. It may not be easy, but it is possible for us, or God would not have made it a requirement for eternal life.

I know that I have trouble grasping reality, yet it is important to me that I experience life through my physical senses, or I would completely lose touch with reality. What I experience is often not real. How can I know that what God says is real and I can trust? What I experience of life and with my senses tells me that there has to be more to this world than what I can taste, touch, smell, see, and feel emotionally.

An ancient writing of the apostle John says, "In the beginning was the Word, and the Word was with God, and the Word was God." (John 1:1). Yahweh is a God of his word. He spoke, and everything came into existence. I have to take God at his word that what I know is true and certain. I may not be able to fully rationalize it, but that doesn't mean it isn't real. If God says his love is true and genuine, that's good enough for me.

In the same way I trust God to be a God of his word, I can trust my mom that when she says she loves me she does. I am past the anger now and know that, if my mom could, she would take away all my pain. In fact she endured great pain that I might come into this world. I know that she endures even greater pain with the realization that her son suffers pain every day and she would gladly take it upon herself if God would have her do that. But my pain is not for my mother to bear; it is mine. I cannot bear the pain that my children might experience in their life, but if I could, I would make it easier for them and take away any fear they may experience. However much I am willing to endure more than just my pain, it is not in God's plan. His plan is that his son, Jesus, bears our pain.

It's knowing that Jesus will take on himself the pain of the whole world that we might have life everlasting is proof enough that I can believe in him. When I am hurt and confused and sorrow twists me inside out, all I need to do is turn it over to him. Why does God allow us to experience pain in the first place? We are made in his image. We are capable of experiencing all that God experiences. This should comfort us because God knows what we are capable of bearing, and he is there with his hands outstretched waiting for us to turn over all the bad and evil in our lives to him, so he might cast it into the deepest ocean.

That doesn't mean we will live our entire lives without experiencing pain and grief again and again. But it does mean that, when we experience it, we can hand it over to him and know his peace and joy. He yearns for us to trust him, for he is our parent too.

FORGETFULNESS

17 May

In yesterday's entry I got on a high horse, so to speak, and preached. Today I wonder why I hadn't thought of what I preached before my attempt to take my life. It's not like God wasn't there; he was. The darkness inside me blinded me to his light, and I panicked. The only comfort I have is that he did not panic with me. He is the shepherd, and I am the sheep. One thing about sheep is they are shortsighted. They need guidance, or they would get lost and wander off. Sometimes the shepherd has to pick up the sheep and carry them over the hard places in the terrain. That's what God did for me. He knew it wasn't my time to die.

One of the issues that I deal with is forgetfulness. When I set my legs on fire in 1983, the burns to my legs did more than just physical damage to my skin, muscle, and nerve tissue. My blood pressure soared resulting in some brain damage. When I talk, I find it difficult to find the words that I want to use to express an idea or thought. I don't seem to have the same problem when I write. I forget things that I do and have to be reminded of them later, or I would make even greater errors and problems for myself. That is why I try to remember to write everything of importance down as it occurs, so I have a record for later reference.

Red Boat
Oil, 22 × 28 inches
2003

On the previous page (p. 91), *Red Boat* represents a peaceful and serene scene on the coast of Crete. It's the off-season for fishing, and the fishing boats are up on the shore on blocks. It's also off-season for the tourists, so it's a hot, lazy day in this coastal village. The red boat is anchored on the water waiting for some villager to take it out for a relaxing fishing trip out in the cove. Based on the sun's light, it is about three o'clock in the afternoon, in the middle of the siesta. That's why there is no one outside in the scene. The church roof has a bright-red hue like the boat, whereas the shadows have a blue-violet hue. Each of the boats on the beach has a different coloration expressing variety and individuality. When I consider the magnitude of God, I know that he is infinite in his ability to create. His imagination is beyond imagination. All of creation has a place of rest in his world.

This painting is titled *Pool Mom* and is a portrait of my mother. It is not meant to be negative. I attempted to capture the agitation that sometimes exists between us. We both are headstrong and often do not mean to get into arguments, but this is the consequence of being from two different generations and having different values with respect to the times in which we were raised. Her generation, coming out of the depression and World War II era, valued money as a necessity and security, whereas my generation saw it as having an economic stranglehold on society and devalued its importance along with the accumulation of wealth. We spent it like we would never run out of it.

UP FROM THE ASHES

18 May

I have a picture of a wood sculpture I created titled *Fish, Flame and Feathered Friend*. It is a chainsaw carving out of African mahogany that I made while studying at Goshen College. I mounted it on a steel post that you would find in a parking garage and welded a transmission rod on top of it. The wood is carved with the main section looking like a fish on an angler's fishing line. On the end of the fish's tail is the form of a single flame like you might see on a candle. This sculpture represents the phoenix experience that I went through while studying at Goshen College. I arose from the ashes of my life and excelled at everything I set my mind to accomplish. The fish form in the sculpture signifies Jesus's miracle of the loaves and fishes, and his supply for all my needs. The flame is suggestive of what I went through in West Germany at the army hospital, with the added meaning of purifying my spirit and preparing me for this transition in my life.

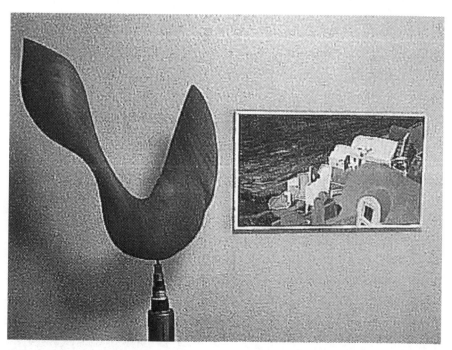

21 May

Lady of the Lake
Oil, 24 × 36 inches
1998

I have done three paintings of my daughter. *Lady of the Lake* I did from sketches and a photograph of her sitting on the rocks on the edge of Lake Michigan near Sault Ste. Marie in the northern peninsula of Michigan. As a child, she was very precocious and stubborn. She wouldn't let her mom pick out any of her clothes when they went shopping. She remains fairly independent to this day, but now she's a mom too, with a daughter that is just like her.

I talked on the phone with my son today. We scheduled for me to come down to where he lives in Peru, Indiana and go out to eat. It has been a month and a half since our last get together. Our relationship has been strained since the divorce from his mother but I thought I should take a risk and see if we could get together. He was very accommodating, and our conversation was brief but friendly.

Since I have had little communication with my family, I don't know how much I should do in initiating contact. As I see it, they cut me off, and if they want to resume a relationship, they will need to take the first step. However, my son did meet with me on Easter with my grandson for breakfast, so I felt somewhat comfortable in calling him.

Below is the only portrait I did of him when he was a senior in high school. He is a laid-back person and very cool. The autumn scene seemed to fit him for the pose. He was the only one of the family that chose to attend church when the rest of us had basically given up in finding one that we felt at home with.

Despite my example as a father, my son turned out to be levelheaded and wise. He isn't driven by the passions that have controlled me most of my life. He decided early in his high school years what he wanted to do as an adult, and he made a plan to accomplish just that. Now he is a computer programmer for a local bank in Marion, Indiana. He has also started his own Internet business designing websites for small businesses and churches.

I am glad that he didn't inherit my propensity for mental health issues. Both his sister and he are very stable and of good mental health.

CHANCE MEETING OR SOMETHING ELSE

27 May

I met my sister at Wal-Mart this afternoon. She had not talked to me since my attempted suicide six and a half months ago. She seemed happy to see me. We mostly talked small talk. Her dog was at the vet getting snipped, so she had to go. I don't know exactly how I feel about our brief time together. There is a mixture of sadness, anger, frustration, and longing. I want to have a relationship with her, but I don't know what strings would be attached. Do I have to behave myself? Can we talk about things that are important to me? I guess I should be happy that she didn't turn and run when she saw me; that's at least a positive step forward.

There are not a lot of people in my life. I always thought our family was tight-knit, but I have come to realize that was a delusion. The true nature of our family emerged when I tried to kill myself. I don't know if we can ever be a family like I thought and felt we were. Some people have absolutely no relationship with their family, or they have no family at all, or they have relationships with nonfamily persons that they look upon as their family.

I went on the Internet and did a search for sites that were for people like me, with bipolar and schizoaffective disorder. There are a number of sites where you can blog or connect with people like me. I read through some of the entries but didn't respond or add my own entry. There is something disconnected about communicating through the Internet medium. Too many of the entries were about how they felt or thought. I could identify, but I want more of a relationship than just a few lines that sit there forever for people to caulk over.

Talking about how one feels and thinks is necessary and important. Still, the conversation has to be productive and moving on past the immediate emotional and cognitive garbage that's going on inside. Some people on the site talked about how they had lost interest in those things that once gave them satisfaction and pleasure. I can relate to that. I haven't done my art for several years, and I once enjoyed reading a lot. I gave up on my art partly because it ceased to function for me as it once had but also because I had no place to put it anymore. I was renting storage space; however, that got to be too expensive, and the people I gave it to had enough. I had the ambition of selling my work, but few showed any interest in paying me what it was worth.

A lot of people have the same attitude about the arts as they have about sex: you shouldn't have to pay for it.

Whether I create a painting or write a book, I do it in part for the satisfaction. I also do it to make a living. There should be some value in the effort that I put forth to create a thing. But people think God created the world we live in and he didn't ask one red cent for his effort and labor. He just gave it away for others to exploit.

One of the things in my head when I tried to kill myself was I had no value anymore. People didn't care about my labor and effort. Why should I go on creating and living if my life has no value to others? I can't help but still feel and think that way still. I am still fragile in some respects. The only thing that keeps me together part of the time is the hope that my family's faith in me will be restored.

I can't just think of myself, even though it may seem that is all I do. When I attempted suicide, I broke with the faith that most people hold dear, that life is precious. It's difficult for most people to conceive that some people would be so depressed that they would think their life is meaningless and hopeless. When that faith is broken, it is like the one you love committed the unpardonable sin. That person has forever broken the relationship with God, so it only is logical that that person has broken the relationship with humanity as a whole. I don't have an answer to comfort people who believe that life is worth living no matter how bad it may seem or restore their faith in me. I know that God still loves me and wants to have a relationship with me; they have to come to that point also in their thinking. However, it is difficult to do. Our society condemns those who break that covenant with life and God; to the majority of people the person who attempts or commits suicide has caused them unforgiveable pain. Society as whole thinks that if a person sees no value in life, then why should it see value in that person.

Maybe I am wrong in my understanding of how society and people think of people who have done what I have tried to do. I have been wrong about a lot of things in my life, some because of my wrong thinking, other things because I simply don't think like the majority of people around me.

Getting Over It
Oil, 30 × 40 inches
2004

    The painting above is titled *Getting Over It*. It was the last painting I completed before admitting myself in the VA hospital in 2004. I had been obsessed with assassinating the then sitting president of the United States but had come to the realization that I would not succeed. I began thinking about how I could make the attempt and force the president's secret service to kill me. Eventually, my thoughts simply turned to ways I could end my life. The process of my thoughts spanned over four months. I was so obsessed that I did not even once think about how my obsession if taken to its ultimate conclusion would affect others. I was consumed by a whole range of emotions.

    At the lower left corner of the painting, I depicted a hollow-point bullet coming out of the canvas. I also painted a spiral to signify how my thoughts were racing and spinning out of control. The mannequin figures represent feelings at different points of my processing of thoughts during this manic-depressive episode. It is probably the strongest of the eight paintings that I painted for an abstract series. Four paintings I had created before my admission the hospital, and four I created after my discharge and on medication for psychosis and depression. The central patch of color is a bone color and is painted to represent how deep my thoughts were—to the core of my being. It was because of this painting and my meditation on it that I came to realize that I needed help. I wanted to end my life, but I still held a small degree of hope that someone could help me out of the way my thoughts had developed.

Just as with my Greek series painting, I seek to balance several painting techniques: such as brushwork, palette-knife scraping, dripping, pouring, and staining. All of these techniques put together ways in communicating my thoughts and emotions. Circles and curved arks represent the different ideas and their relationship to other ideas. They are within and overlapping each other, just like our relationship with people in our lives.

I have another thought about meeting my sister this afternoon. It was a chance encounter; but was it fate that we met? I was about done with my shopping when turning a corner of an isle in the store, and there was my sister. Maybe God meant for us to meet. Maybe he wanted me to face my emotions and see how I would relate to my sister in the face of them. While they were disturbing to me, I think and feel I handled the situation the best that I could.

So much of what we experience in our lives is chance or fate. Life gives us little tests to see how we will handle them. Are we successful, or do we fail? There is not necessarily a right of wrong answer to the test but an opportunity. Jesus encountered many people during the three years of his ministry: a woman who was about to be stoned, a crowd of hungry people by the Sea of Galilee, a poor woman who gave of her last two pence as a tithe, and so many more. Were those encounters fate or chance? How did he handle those situations? The scriptures paint a perfect portrait, and so can we.

THIS TOO WILL PASS

September 24

I chose today to include another entry in this diary. Since I am self-publishing this diary but don't have the funds to do so, I put it on hold. On August 26, I was in an auto accident, and according to what my family has told me, I was at fault. For some unknown reason, I crossed the center line and struck a truck head on. When I woke up after being in a coma until September 3, I had no memory of the event. There has been a lot of speculation from I was committing suicide to I had a seizure. The first reason seems unlikely since I was on my way to the Fort Wayne VA hospital and was looking forward to it. I hadn't any thoughts of suicide prior to the accident. The seizure rationale seems the most likely one, for I have a history of seizures starting in April 2009. It had been almost six months since my last seizure, but because I have no memory of the incident, no one really knows. My last memory before the accident was I was driving south, out of Goshen, near the city's VA clinic. Then I woke up in the intensive care unit of the hospital.

The fact that I survived the collision is itself a miracle. My injuries included a compound fracture to my left arm that they at first thought would have to be amputated but were able to save, a simple fracture to my right wrist, and a fracture to my C6 vertebra. My left hand is partially paralyzed from the nerve damage. Part of me wonders whether this is the continuation of the curse I am under; however, I have come to think and feel that my survival is testament to God's grace.

Since my last entry in this diary back in May, I have felt the hand of God directing my life. I have had renewed interest in joining a fellowship of believers. Other things have taken place that I had no control over. The condo that my wife and I owned finally sold. The buyers stuck with us as we tried to get the two mortgage companies that lent us money for the purchase of the home come to an agreement on the short sale of the home. They at first resisted our request since it meant they would have to take a loss on the sale of our home, but they finally came around and agreed to a compromise that all parties could accept. I believe that through it all, God was showing me that he was with me working things out, that he had no intention on letting me die before he had completed his work in and through me.

God even provided me the money from the car insurance settlement to pay off a number of my debts and have enough left over to pay for the publication of my diary. I don't know what will be the outcome to publishing it, but I feel he is directing me to move forward with it.

I know I have a long road of recovery ahead of me. The staff at the Marion VA hospital, where I was transferred for rehabilitation, has projected that I will be ready for discharge the first week of November. I am still in a lot of pain from my injuries, and it's difficult to see that far ahead just yet. I know that this too will pass.

FORTIETH DAY

15 November

This is the last diary entry in my diary. When I started this diary, I was going to call it *Fourteen Days from the Diary of Delusional Man*. After the first reading by the editorial staff of my publisher, they informed me that it was too short and that I needed to add more pages. So I set a new goal for the diary and decided to title it *Forty Days from the Diary of Delusional Man: Revelations and Meditations*. I don't think that I repeated myself too often during the writing of the diary, but I may have.

Those who read this diary will be the final critics and judges to the value of the diary's content. Like I said before in the diary, my life is split into two parts, each of approximately twenty-six years. This diary has been in process for a long time; it took an inspired moment to write down what I felt was important to say. Whether I am judged to be delusional or not is not for me to say but those who read it. I hope that many will benefit from what I have written here. It is not my intent to speak hurtfully of those who have contributed to my life's story. I believe God had a purpose for each person who came in contact with me, not for good or evil but just to be.

I believe that while God has a hand in guiding our lives, the true course of our life is not written until we make choices. It twists and turns through forests, deserts, and meadows. Each life's path is different, but for those who follow Jesus, it is narrow and eventually ends in meeting his Father. Some days I am in a valley and the sky is dark; at other times, I rise over a hill or mountaintop and see the light of the Father in the distance or high overhead. Life is not meant to be the same for each person. That's what makes it interesting and worth living.

I have not always cherished the life I have been given to live. It doesn't make me less or more of a person. I am that I am. If I didn't know great sorrow, then I would not know great joy. In the beginning, God made the sun and the stars and the moon, he separated light from darkness. Such was to be the life of his creation. He meant for us to know sunny days and stormy days, dry days and wet days. Such is to be the life of his creation.

From life's possibilities, I have experienced more than some and less than others. In the end of my life, it will be just right. This I know, and for this reason, I continue to go on.

EPILOGUE

My life has had its share of twists and turns. Could I have made better choices? Maybe. Should I have seen someone about the mental health issues I was dealing with? Probably. There are a lot of *maybes* and *probablys* and, for that matter, *ifs* too, when it comes to my life. But considering all the factors that went into how my life has come to be today, I don't think it could have turned out any different than it has.

I had a dream that caused me to change directions when I was eighteen. It is still as vivid in my mind as when I awoke from the dream. In it I was with a group of believers on a hillside, and there were three other groups of believers: one on a platform, one in a valley, and one on a mountaintop. I cried out in the dream, "It's not too late to serve." But a voice came back, "It will be to late; now is the time to serve." I was living in Dodge City, Kansas at the time, after quitting my work with a wheat harvest crew. The next morning, I sold all my possession, packed a backpack and started walking to Mexico to do mission work. I had not gone more then a mile when the pastor of a church I had been attending the city drove up beside me and asked me what I was doing. After telling him about the dream I had had and the voices telling me to go to Mexico he took me to his church and had me call my dad, who was hunting in Colorado. He came and picked me up the next day. Two months later, I was in Washington DC working as a volunteer for the Mennonite Church. When I started that road trip, I had the right thing in mind. I was just going in the wrong direction. God turned me around. Way back then, he knew who I was, with all my human fragilities, but he still wanted to work in me and through me. It doesn't make much sense that he would choose someone like me, but he did. How much more could he do with someone who is greater than I in every way?

What was in my heart and mind when I joined the army in 1981 was I wanted to go to college and also to serve. I made the choice that my country told me was the right one. All that stopped me from enlisting in 1975 had fallen away, and the doors were opened. How it would turn out I did not see or envision. It just happened the way it happened. I don't think God wanted it to happen any other way.

Is my life now at an end? I don't know what tomorrow will be or bring, but whatever may come, I know that God's will will be done when it comes to me. I am an imperfect vessel, but for some reason that only he fully knows, it's the perfect vessel for him. Whenever I try to improve on his design, he brings me back to the knowledge that he doesn't necessarily want an improved model but the one he chose to begin with.

More times than I can count, I have prayed to Jesus, "Take this cup from me." God did not send me to be a sacrifice for the sins of the world. I am not Jesus; he by far is greater than I. But like him, I am left with only one thing to say: "Thy will be done." The only choices he really gives us is to submit or to resist. It matters not what we may choose; his will will be done in the end.

We are back to where I began. Could my life have turned out better if I had submitted to his will? The answer I have for that question is no. If I would have given in, submitted to man's will, everything may have gone well for me. I know from where I am today that, while by all appearances and rationale of mankind I have made a whole slew of wrong choices, I would have been resisting his will for my life. The only way he could teach me, show that he loved and believed in me, and work his purpose out was in the choices that he knew I would make. If we seek him out, he will reveal himself to us. This I know.

Appendix

Samplings of Other Artworks

Hanging Chad
Oil, 30 × 40 inches
2005

The Boss's Chair
Oil, 26 × 32 inches
2004

Next Page

Sarasota Sunset
Oil, 14 × 24 inches
2005

On the Chuck Wagon
Oil, 30 × 30 inches
2006

Sunrise, Sunset
Oil, 30 × 40 inches
2007

Landscape 1
Oil, 30 × 40 inches
2007